Dear Jeanette,

Happy Serging!

hugs

Pam
2021

Power Serge

by Pam Damour and Betty Mitchell

Photography: Pam Damour, Betty Mitchell, Erin Busch

Cover design, book layout, and index: Erin Busch

© 2018 Copyright
Pam Damour

**495 Point Au Fer Road
Champlain, NY 12919**

Printed in China

Dedication

Carol Vealy-Ellis

Betty and I learned many of our serger techniques from Carol Vealy-Ellis.

When everyone was using a serger merely to make factory finishes on garments, Carol pushed the envelope trying new ways and new techniques on the serger. She was instrumental in the research and development of many of the serger features used in this book. Always a pioneer, Carol was never afraid to try anything new. Her courage and creativity paved the way for teachers like us and many others. We can't even imagine how many lives Carol has touched through sewing. One of Carol's greatest gifts was her ability to teach patience and understanding which has been invaluable in our teaching profession. Even though she's no longer active in the sewing world, she continues to inspire and support our community. She is sorely missed and deeply admired. Carol is the "wind beneath our wings".

Dearest Carol, this book is dedicated to you!

Contents

 Each project has spools of difficulty ranging from 1-5. *1 being the easiest, 5 being the most difficult.* SAMPLE = DIFFICULTY 2

 Available at pamdamour.com

 Some techniques and projects have video clips or tutorials associated with them. Use a QR code scanner or look for the url addresses on page 28.

Table of Contents

Foreword

Kathy McMakin

Decades have gone by and sergers remain a treasured part of my sewing life. I simply cannot sew without one! Even more astounding are the techniques Pam and Betty have discovered, perfected, and continue to explore in their own serger practices.

A restless, creative, push-the-envelope personality, Pam, with Betty as her accomplice, reveal themselves in this book as technical wizards - always seeking the easiest way to achieve sure-fire success. They, ultimately, share it with all of us!

Filled with great inventive serger projects sure to hone your own serger skills and ramp up your serger confidence, the book brings us projects made easier and better by using accessory feet and attachments. It also contains projects made more creative by incorporating trims, braids, ric-rac and a range of threads, and projects made more sophisticated with the use of all types of serger stitches - rolled hem, narrow and wide overlock, chain and cover stitches, and more. In other words, serger techniques galore!

In a nutshell: "If you own a serger, you'll want to own this book!"

Who is Kathy?

Kathy McMakin, whose own introduction to the serger has been described as "love at first sight" is one of America's foremost authorities in the field of heirloom sewing by machine and by serger. Her long and continuing tenure with the Martha Pullen Company, along with her current role as the Editor of Classic Sewing magazine have allowed her to share her vast skills with sewists from every corner of the world for the past 35 years. Kathy has been an inspiration to sewists internationally and has created a new level of confidence and creative fulfillment.

Kathy and her husband David reside in Birmingham, Alabama. They have two grown children and three absolutely precious grandchildren.

Introduction/Contributors

Introduction

This serger book is designed to help you step out of your comfort zone with your serger. If you haven't experimented with all that your serger can do, try all the finishing techniques and technique blocks first, and put them into a notebook for future reference. Once you've mastered our trims and techniques, incorporate them into all your serging projects. Whether you're a quilter, garment sewist, or crafter, the serger can make your sewing life fun and creative. Because of the generosity of Tacony Corporation, we were able to test out techniques on the Baby Lock sergers. If you own another brand, please refer to your owner's manual for the proper settings. Now is the time to have a love affair with your serger!

Contributors

If you've ever written a book, you can understand how much work and how many changes the book takes before it gets to the printer. We have read and re-read this book, always hoping to send an error-free book to the printers. Reality has proven to us that something always gets missed, so please forgive us for any errors that may slip through the cracks. Without the help of our special friends who helped by testing our directions, and proof reading over and over again, this book would not be possible!

A big thank you goes out to:
Erin Busch, graphic designer
Joanne Sandell, tester and proofer
Carolyn Wells, tester and proofer
Fran Hershfield, proofer
Tammie Gerke, proofer
Diane Billerman, tester and proofer
Audrey Rabideau, tester
Charlie Garrand, model

Who is Pam Damour?

Known as the "Decorating Diva", Pam learned early in life, while spending time on her grandparents' farm, that making something from "scratch" was not only a way of life, but it was the better way of doing things. Holding on to those values, she went from farm to fabric and has had a very successful 30+ year career as an interior designer and sewing professional. Pam offers professional drapery workroom training to the trade and consumers. As a seasoned career speaker, she travels internationally, teaching her specialty techniques that have brought her years of continued business as the "Couture of Home Dec Sewing". She is the author of *Pillow Talk, Cheaper by the Dozen, Got Quilts?, The Tangled Home,* and *Hold Everything.* She is also a producer of 12 Home Dec DVDs, several patterns, and is a designer of notions and templates. An interior designer by profession and a quilter by passion, Pam lives on the shore of Lake Champlain in a log home nestled at the foot of the Adirondack Mountains where she holds sewing retreats and her much sought after Window Treatment Boot Camp. Her down to earth nature, never forgetting her roots, combined with her professionalism, lays the foundation for a warm and creative experience. If you would like to attend one of Pam's events, contact your local sewing store or go to www.pamdamour.com.

Words From the Author

I still remember the day I met Betty Mitchell. We were at a sewing conference (I know, what a surprise!) in Raleigh, North Carolina. I knew immediately we would become great friends, but I never could have imagined what a great asset she would become to my sewing career. In the fourteen years that we have been friends, she has sewn tirelessly for my last five books, she has pushed my creativity to new limits and has made me a better teacher. Of all my dearest sewing friends, she has inspired me the most. Thank you Betty for your friendship, your advice and your guidance.

Hugs & Stitches,
Pam

Who is Betty Mitchell?

Betty Mitchell began her love affair with the sewing machine at the age of eight and it has grown ever since. She spent 30 years in Rhode Island, teaching Family and Consumer Sciences and 'retired' to work for sewing machine dealers in southwest Florida for eight years. During that time, she not only sold machines and taught classes, she also spent three years as a store manager for one of the largest dealers in the country. At the same time, she began teaching at national dealer conventions, various sewing and quilting shows, as well as local and regional sewing guilds. Nine years ago, she re-retired to be with her grandchildren in Kentucky. She continues to teach both locally and nationally. Betty began as a garment sewer, moved on to Home Décor, embroidery and sergers. She has recently returned to her roots in garment construction combining over sixty years of sewing experience into clothing that is unique and on trend. Her classes are meant to be informative and relaxing. Betty says, "In the end, it's just a bunch of thread and fiber to have fun with! If there's a sewing tool or fabric that I haven't met, it's not because I haven't tried. I firmly believe that I'll never have enough fabric and I certainly deserve the best tools."

Words From the Author

So I described the first book, "Hold Everything", as Wow! And for this one – Oh my goodness we did it again! I have been using a serger and teaching others how to use them for over thirty years. I believe, and hope to inspire in my students, that sewing on a serger can be just as creative and fun as using a conventional sewing machine. Sew, relax, and spread your creative wings!

Thank you Pam for knowing I could do this and for all the pushes and inspiration along the way. And to my greatest cheerleaders – Josh and Matt – always remember that the hard things, the ones you never thought you could do, will reap the most rewards and are worth every effort to accomplish.

Sew in Peace,
Betty

Serger Pointers

Basic information for all brands

- Since you cannot back stitch on a serger, see your owner's manual for information on securing thread tails. There are several methods and you need to find those you like best.
- When stitching in the round (like hemming a T-shirt), overlap your stitching for an inch or more at the end.
- Test sew decorative threads on same fabric to determine proper stitch length. If you begin with a stitch that is too short, you are likely to get thread jams.
- If you have a serger without cover or chain stitch capability, or a Baby Lock Imagine or Enlighten, you can always use your sewing machine for decorative stitches. If stitching on the inside of the project pieces you can use bobbin work on your sewing machine with heavy thread wound on the bobbin. Try decorative stitches or thread couching on the top side of the project pieces as a replacement for cover and chain stitching.
- When cover stitch or chain stitch are used for basic sewing, you can replace the with straight stitching on your sewing machine.

Basic Baby Lock Information

- Cover stitch always starts on fabric.
- If you have an Imagine without the wave stitch, you can use a rolled edge or 3-thread overlock - wide with heavy thread in the loopers to replace the wave stitch. Choice is determined by amount of coverage you desire.
- See Basic Information if you have an Imagine or Enlighten and need to replace cover or chain stitches.

Other Serger Brands

- Rolled edge or 3-thread overlock wide can replace the wave stitch – your choice depends on width of stitching desired.
- While this book features Baby Lock sergers, it can easily be adapted for any serger with the following considerations: you will need to know how to adjust the tensions on your serger. Please remember that on sergers with manual tension adjustments the numbers given are guidelines and not "cast in concrete". For example, if all tensions are recommended at 4, you may need something like 4, 4.1, 3.75 or 4.25.
- Along with your manual, the following guide should help you balance your tensions:
  - 4-thread: all tensions are usually the same
  - 3-thread overlock - wide: lower the upper looper tension by 1
  - 3-thread overlock - narrow: all the same as 4-thread overlock
  - Rolled edge: upper looper is loosened; lower looper is tighter, the difference between these two numbers will be 5 or more
- For specialty serger feet, consult your dealer, owner's manual, or the manufacturer of your serger.

For threading non-Baby Lock sergers

If you own a serger that does not have an automatic threading system, you will be doing yourself a great favor if you do not thread your serger by tying on threads. Taking the time to learn to thread your loopers from start to finish will actually save you time in the future. If you only know how to thread by tying on to the previous threads and a thread breaks where there isn't enough thread remaining to tie on, you will now end up with your owner's manual in your lap trying to figure out how to fix it. Take a week and cut the threads every day, rethread and test sew. Each day you will work faster and by the end of the week you will never have to tie on again

Please Note: In the beginning of writing this book, it was our wish to make an "All Inclusive Brands" book, but after two years of asking for loaner machines from the different companies, we are only using the company that did provide a loaner serger for this book. Although we do own other brands in our sewing studios, and we respect all brands, we need to keep the technology current with machines and setting that are available at press time.

Block Techniques

Block Techniques

Basket Weave Block by Pam

The belt loop attachment for your serger is great for making belt loops and so much more! It makes a great trim which can embellish the edge of a project, be an applied trim, or woven together to create fabric. This block is woven with large and small belt loop strips, but you can make them all one size if you prefer.

Note: For this technique, you will need a serger with a cover stitch.

Supplies

- ⅞" bias cut strips (about 110" total)
- 1⅝" bias cut strips (about 70" total)
- Small belt loop folder attachment
- Large belt loop folder attachment
- Three spools of serger cone thread
- Brass stiletto 🧷
- 7" square of Fantastic Fusible Fabric Backing® 🧷
- Painter's or masking tape

Cover Stitch - Wide
Needle Position: Right, Left
Stitch Width: N/A
Stitch Length: 3.0
Stitch Selector: N/A
Differential: 1.0 or N
Foot: Curve Foot
Cutter: Locked

Construction

- Do not sew bias strips together. They are easier to sew if inserted into the attachment as needed.

- Set up your serger for a cover stitch - wide using the listed settings.

- Cut your bias strip to a point for easier insertion.

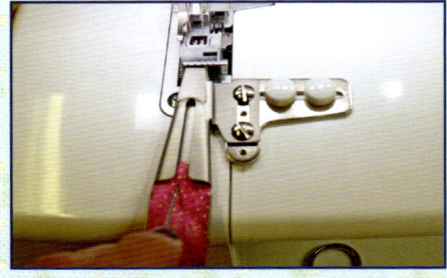

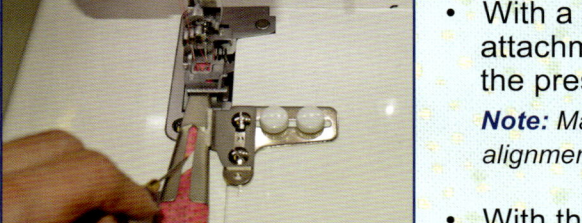

- With a stiletto, feed your bias strip with the right side up into the attachment. Pull the strip through the attachment so that it is under the presser foot and has contact with the feed teeth.
  Note: Make a 6" test sample first to make sure your attachment is in correct alignment.

- With thread tails pulled to the back, start slowly until your serger is stitching the fabrics.

- If the stitches are an equal distance from each folded edge, continue with the rest of the bias. If stitches are unequal distances, loosen the thumb screws slightly to adjust to the right or left as needed.

- To add additional bias strips, use your stiletto to slide the next strip under the existing strip in the attachment.

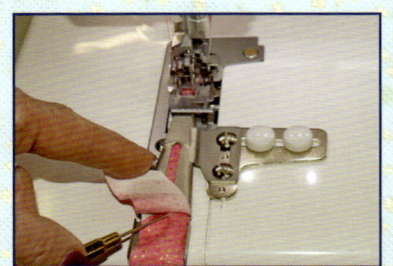

- Hold it in place as the serger takes both layers at one time.

Block Techniques

Construction (CONTINUED)

- You will need a total of 91" of small bias belt loop and 56" of wide belt loop.

- Cut the belt loops into 7" sections.

- On a pressing/pinning surface, place your 7" square of Fantastic Fusible Fabric Backing® with the wrong (fusible) side up.

- Secure the top edge of the backing with pins. Secure the bottom edge of the fusible backing with painter's tape.

- Starting at the top, pin the 8 - 7" pieces of wide bias along the top edge of the Fantastic Fusible Fabric Backing®.

- Lift every other wide bias strip and lay one of the narrow strips, butting them up to the pins at the top edge of the Fantastic Fusible Fabric Backing®.

- Add the second horizontal strip, lifting the alternate vertical strips.

- Repeat these last two rows, creating a basket weave pattern.

- When the block is complete, tape the edges with painter's tape to keep the strips from shifting.

- Press the entire block with full steam until all the pieces are secured to the Fantastic Fusible Fabric Backing®.

3-Thread Overlock – Wide

Stitch Width: 5.5
Stitch Length: 3.0
Stitch Selector: A
Differential: 1.0 or N
Foot: Curve Foot

- Convert the serger to a 3-thread overlock - wide with a width of 5.5 and serge the edges, trimming the block to a 6½" square.

Block Techniques

Box Pleated Windows Block by Pam

Pleated Windows, which resemble Cathedral Windows in quilts are a great insert in any sewing project. The fabric MUST be cut on the bias for the pleats to fold back softly.

Supplies

- Bias strip of fabric cut 7" wide by 22"
- Box Pleat Tape®
- One spool of Lamé Stylo Thread
- Three cones of serger thread

Construction

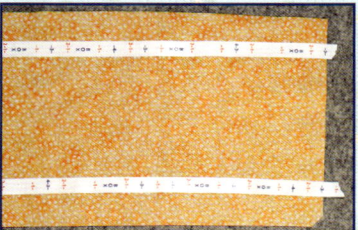

- Set serger for a 3-thread overlock - wide

- Place tape on each side, about 1 to 1½" from the outside edges, lining up the numbers on each side. For more details on how to make box pleat, see page 37.

3-Thread Overlock – Wide	
Needle Position:	Left
Stitch Width:	6.0
Stitch Length:	3.0
Stitch Selector:	A
Differential:	1.0 or N
Foot:	Curve Foot

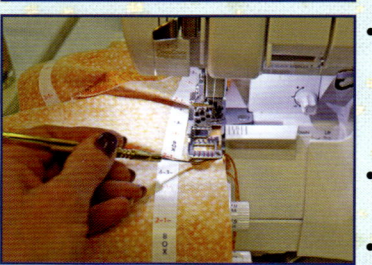

- Using the cone thread, pleat fabric 2", using the directions on the Box Pleat Tape® package. Stitch both edges down, barely trimming on each side.

- Remove tape.

- Press pleats flat.

Chain Stitch	
Needle Position:	Center
Stitch Width:	N/A
Stitch Length:	2.5 to 3.0
Stitch Selector:	N/A
Differential:	1.0 or N
Foot:	Cover/Chain

- Convert to a chain stitch.

- Sew down the center from the wrong side using a chain stitch to the secure windows. This will put the heavy chain (pretty) stitching on the right sides. (If you do not have a cover/chain stitch on your serger, use a straight stitch on your sewing machine.)

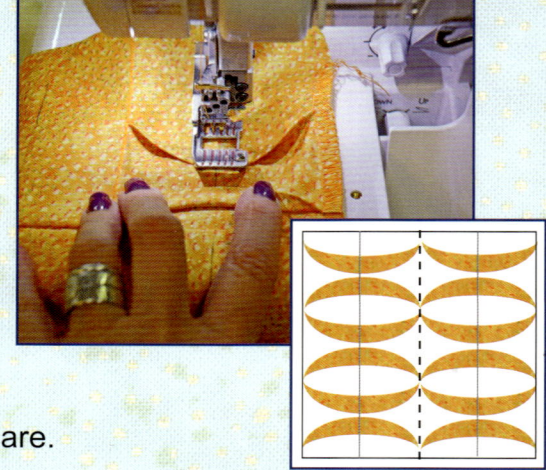

- Flip over to the right side, and fold each pleat back in the opposite direction and stitch from the right side with matching or invisible thread, stitching down the center of each side.

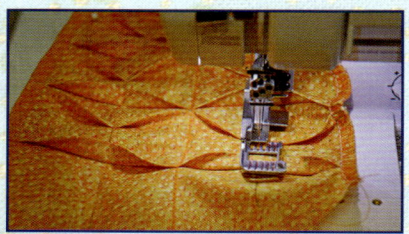

- Press flat. Trim to 6½" square.

Block Techniques

Chain Stitch Ruffle Block by Betty

Rolled edges, gathering and some ribbon or trim create a versatile and easy accent. Just picture this on the edge of a towel, the hem of a skirt, or set vertically on the front of a dress or shirt.

Supplies

- 7½" square of base fabric
- 2½" x 18" coordinating fabric for the ruffle
- Madeira Aeroflock or other decorative thread for the rolled edge
- Three cones of serger thread to coordinate with the decorative thread
- 10" of ½" wide ribbon or trim
- Cover/chain stitch foot

Rolled Edge

Needle Position: Right Overlock
Wave/Overlock: Overlock
Stitch Width: 3.5
Stitch Length: 1.0
Stitch Selector: D
Differential: N
Foot: Utility foot

Construction

- Thread the serger for a 3-thread rolled edge with the decorative thread in the upper looper.

- Test the rolled edge on a scrap of fabric to determine the stitch length needed for the decorative thread you have selected (the heavier the thread, the longer the stitch).

- Stitch a rolled edge on both long sides of the ruffled fabric.

- Using serger cone thread, thread the serger for a center needle chain stitch.

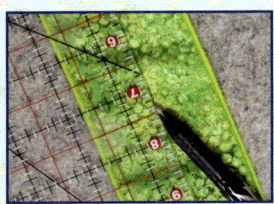

- Mark a stitching line centered on the length of the ruffle fabric.

- Attach the cover/chain stitch foot and adjust your differential feed to 2 and your stitch length to 2.

- Chain stitch on this line, gathering the ruffle as you stitch.

- Place the ruffle diagonally on the base square.

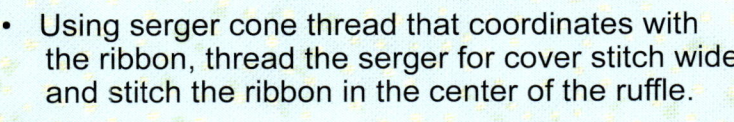

- Attach using the center needle chain stitch after adjusting the stitch length and differential as described.

- Using serger cone thread that coordinates with the ribbon, thread the serger for cover stitch wide and stitch the ribbon in the center of the ruffle.

- Square the block to 6½" x 6½".

Chain Stitch

Needle: Center Needle Position
Stitch Width: N/A
Stitch Length: 4.0
Stitch Selector: N/A
Differential: 2
Foot: Cover/Chain
To Attach Ruffle:
Stitch Length: 2
Differential: N

Cover Stitch - Wide

Needle: Left, Right
Stitch Width: N/A
Stitch Length: 2.5-3.0
Stitch Selector: N/A
Differential: N

Block Techniques

Circles and Squares Block by Betty

Chain and cover stitching using decorative thread in the looper creates beautiful decorative fabric. It is basically bobbin work on the serger. Stitching on the wrong side of the fabric produces a heavier braided effect on the right side. This block also features serger piecing techniques with a square and quarter square triangles.

Supplies

- 5" square for center of block
- 5" square cut into ¼ square triangles
- 7" square of fusible tear away stabilizer
- Two spools of heavy contrasting decorative thread
- 7 Corner Ruler® by the Sew Sisters

Construction

- Thread serger for 4-thread overlock stitch using serger cone thread.

- Using a ¼" seam allowance, attach a triangle to the opposite sides of the center square.

- Press seams toward the triangles.

- Repeat for the other two triangles.

- Fuse tear away stabilizer to the back of the block.

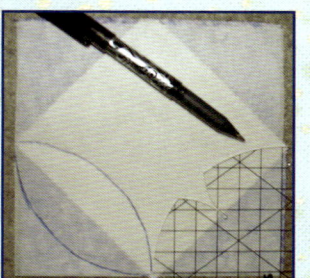

- Using the 3" curve on the 7 Corner Ruler®, draw curves on the back of the square, aligning the curve of the ruler with the corners of the center square.

- Thread the serger for center needle chain stitch with decorative thread in the chain stitch looper.

- Stitch on the curved lines in the center square, beginning and ending at the corners of the inner square.

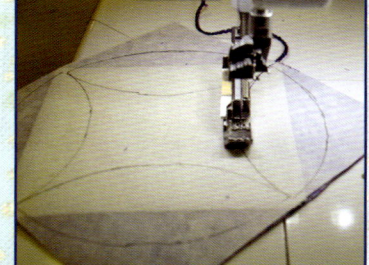

- Change the thread in the looper to the other color.

- Stitch the curves on the ¼ square triangle pieces again, beginning and ending at the corners of the center square and press.

- Square the block to 6 ½" x 6 ½".

4-Thread Overlock

Needle: Left, Right
Wave/Overlock: Overlock
Stitch Width: 6.0
Stitch Length: 2.5
Stitch Selector: A
Differential: N

Chain Stitch

Needle: Center
Stitch Width: N/A
Stitch Length: 3.0
Stitch Selector: N/A
Differential: N

Block Techniques

Cover Stitch Plaid Block by Betty

This technique is 'sew' easy! It can be used to enhance any fabric in any part of a project. Stitching lines can be spaced however you wish and the thread colors can be varied to create different effects. This is basically bobbin work on the serger. Stitching on the wrong side of the fabric produces a heavier braided effect on the right side.

NOTE: If you do not have cover stitch capability, you can achieve a similar effect with a narrow flatlock stitch on the right side of the fabric.

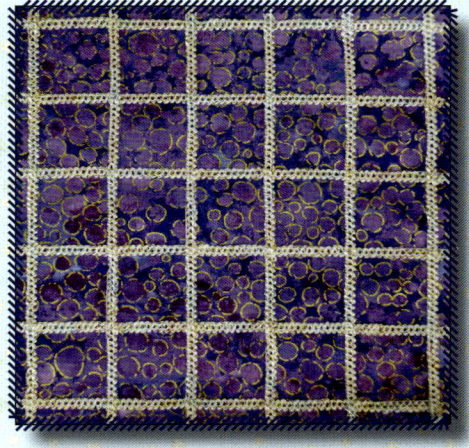

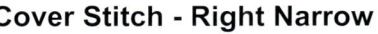

Supplies

- 7 ½" square of fabric
- Heavy decorative thread. (WonderFil™ Dazzle™ is used for this sample)
- Cover chain stitch foot
- Quilting bar (If your serger has one.)
- One cone of serger thread to match decorative thread.

Cover Stitch - Right Narrow
Needle: Center, Right
Stitch Width:
Stitch Length: 3.0
Stitch Selector: A
Differential: N
Heavy decorative thread in chain stitch looper

Construction

- Thread the serger for cover stitch - right narrow. Attach the cover chain stitch foot.

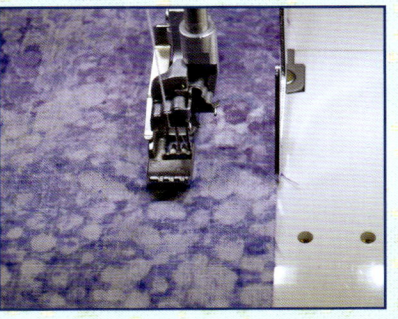

- Attach the quilting bar and set it 1" from the center needle.

- Stitch on the wrong side of the fabric.

- For the first row, align the raw edge of the fabric with the quilting bar.

- If the fabric puckers from the stitching, lower the differential to 0.8.

- For each succeeding row, align the quilting bar with the left side of the previous row.

- As you stitch each new row, keep a finger from your left hand on the beginning thread tail to keep it from curling back and getting caught in your new row.

- Use scissors to trim thread tails as you stitch.

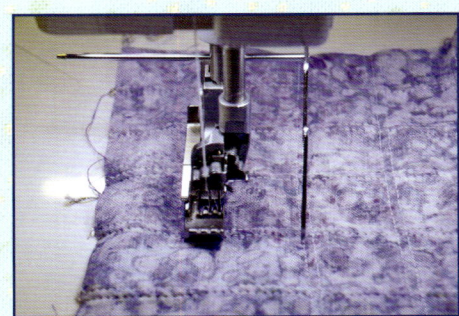

- Continue stitching until you have reached the other side of the block.

- Rotate the block 90° and repeat the above directions to complete the grid.

- Trim the block to a 6 ½" square.

Block Techniques

Decorative Trim Block by Pam

This block is a medley of some of our favorite trims. Combined in one block are the braided rolled edge, wave stitch piping, and double rolled edge piping. If your serger does not have the wave stitch, you can substitute with a 3-thread wide overlock with a shortened stitch, just as we did with the double piping.

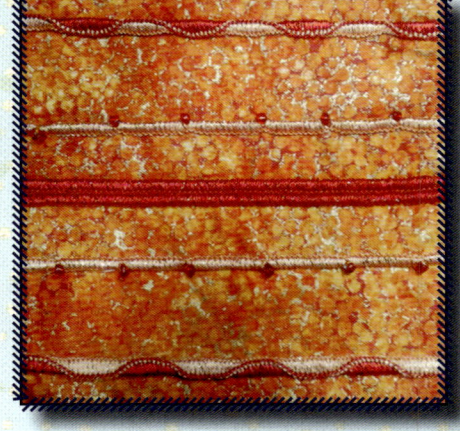

Supplies

- Three spools of WonderFil™ Razzle™ (or other 8 weight thread)
- Two spools of serger thread
- 12-pound fishing line
- Optional: Box Pleat Tape® for the beaded rolled edge
- 12 decorative beads

url on page 28

3-Thread Rolled Edge
Needle: Overlock Position 1
Stitch Width: 5.5
Stitch Length: 1.5
Stitch Selector: D
Differential Feed: 1.0 or N (normal)
Foot: Utiliity and cording/piping
Cutter: Locked

Construction

- For this block, we started with the double piping technique.
  Note: Scan the above QR code for a video tutorial on how to make double piping.

- Fold your square in half with ¼" extending on one side.

- Place the folded edge under the utility foot on your serger with the longer side up.

- Serge 3-thread rolled edge along fold.

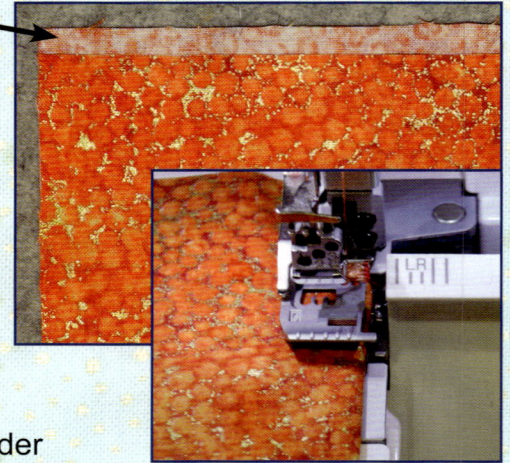

- Press a crease on the longer side ¼" from your previous stitching.

- Place the previous stitching under the groove of your piping foot.

- Serge another row of stitches and press flat.

- Press a fold, with wrong sides together, one inch out from the double piping and sew a beaded rolled edge. (See page 30.)

- Press another fold one inch out and serge a wave stitch along the fold. (See page 41 for wave stitch instructions).

- Trim the block to a 6 ½" square.

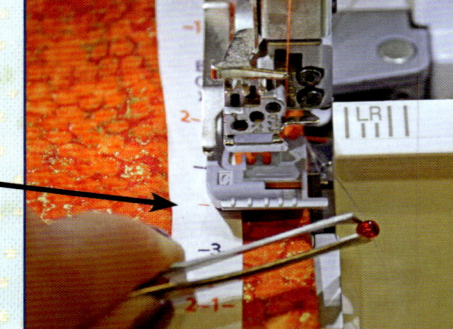

Block Techniques

Flatlock Lace Block   by Betty

Flatlock is one of the oldest decorative techniques for the serger. It is an unbalanced stitch. The stitch is used on a fold of fabric or to secure two cut edges. The tension on the needle thread is so loose that the folded or adjoining fabric can be pulled flat. The top side of the stitch looks similar to an overlock stitch that is not set on the edge of the fabric. The back side of the stitch looks like a ladder.

Supplies
- 7½" square of fabric
- ¾ yard of lace edging
- ½ yard of ⅛" wide ribbon
- Two spools or cones of thread. (machine embroidery thread was used)
- Bind hem foot
- Large double eyed needle

Construction
Ribbon
- Thread the serger for a 2-thread flatlock - wide stitch.

- Using the blind hem foot helps to control this stitch.

- With the wrong side out, fold the fabric in thirds on the lengthwise grain of the fabric. Finger press the folds in place.

2-Thread Flatlock - Wide
Needle: Left Overlock
Stitch Width: 7.5
Stitch Length: 2.5
Stitch Selector: B
Differential Feed: N
Engage Subsidiary Looper

- You will need to practice first to determine how far to move the fabric to the right of the needle. With this sample, the fold was along the right edge of the blind hem foot and the guide on the foot was moved up against the right side of the foot.

- With the wrong side out, stitch along one of the folded edges.

- Stitch the second folded edge. Pull the folds open and press flat.

- Using a large double eyed needle, weave the ribbon through the ladder stitches on the right side of the fabric. Over two under one works well for this technique. Press.

Lace
- Thread the serger for a 2-thread flatlock - narrow stitch.

- Adjust the guide on the blind hem foot by moving it about 1/16" to the right.

- With the right side of the fabric facing out, fold the fabric into fourths. Finger press the folds in place.

- Align the finished edge of the lace with the first fold. Stitch in place just catching the fold and the edge of the lace.

- Open flat and press.

- Stitch the lace on the other two folds in the same manner. Press.

2-Thread Flatlock - Narrow
Needle: Right Overlock
Stitch Width: 5
Stitch Length: 2.5
Stitch Selector: B
Differential Feed: N
Engage Subsidiary Looper

- Trim the completed square to 6½" x 6½".

Block Techniques

Pintucks Block by Pam

Pintucks are an excellent way to add texture and embellishment to your serger projects. One way to achieve perfect pintucks is to use a foot designed for this technique. The deep groove in the foot, combined with the twin needles of cover stitch, make pintucks a snap! With light weight fabrics, the raised ridge of the tuck will form easily, but with heavier home-dec type fabrics, you may need to insert a cord designed for pintucks.

Supplies

- 8" square of fabric
- Pintuck foot with guides
- Pintuck cord (for heavier fabrics)
- Three spools of thread of your choice. (This sample was made with decorative thread in the needles.)

url on page 28

Cover Stitch Right - Narrow	
Needle:	Center, Right
Stitch Width:	N/A
Stitch Length:	2.5
Stitch Selector:	N/A
Differential Feed:	1.0 or N
Foot:	Pintuck with guides

Construction

- Set up your serger for cover stitch right - narrow.

- Always test a scrap of same weight fabric first. If you need more pintucks, add the guide or pintuck cord.

- If you want a definitive pattern, draw it out on the right side of your fabric with a fabric marking pen, or you can follow a design in the fabric.

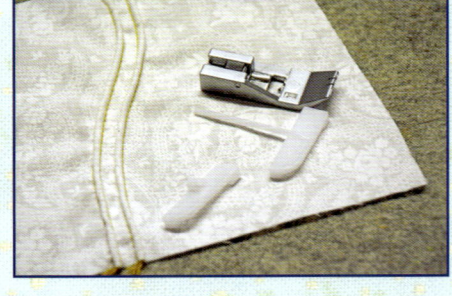

- Always test on a sample fabric first to determine if pintuck cord is needed.

- Remember to cut your fabric larger than needed because the more pintucks you add, the more the fabric will shrink.

Note: Scan the above QR code for a video tutorial on how to make pintucks.

Pintucks Using Rolled Edge

If your serger does not have a cover stitch or if you prefer to make your pintucks with the rolled edge, follow instructions provided on the Heirloom Pillowcase on page 88 for an alternative method.

Rolled Edge Stitch	
Needle:	Right
Stitch Width:	N/A
Stitch Length:	N/A
Stitch Selector:	D
Differential Feed:	1.0 or N
Foot:	Open Toe or Utility

Block Techniques

Prairie Points Block **by Betty**

Serger prairie points are created with squares of fabric that have been folded in half. Decorative stitches are applied along the folded edge, in this case the wave stitch was used. (A 3-thread overlock - wide can be used if your serger does not have the wave stitch.) Two spools of Madeira Decora 12 (one solid and one variegated) were used in the loopers for the sample. The decorative edge is then folded toward the center creating triangles.

url on page 28

Supplies

- One cone of serger thread for the needle
- 2½" x 18" strip of fabric for prairie points
- 9" x 8" coordinating fabric for quilt square
- Two spools Madeira Decora 12 for the loopers

Construction

- For the wave stitch, it is important to remember that the needle is placed in the right needle position, but the thread travels through the left needle tension and the upper looper thread passes through the right needle tension.

- The stitch length is important for proper coverage. The heavier the thread the longer the stitch. It is important to test stitch length before creating your prairie points.

- Fold a 2½" strip of fabric in half and stitch on the folded edge. Use variegated thread in the upper looper and a solid color in the lower looper.

- Cut the strip every 2½" to form rectangles that are 2½" x 1¼".

- Fold the decorative edge toward the center forming a triangle and press edges.

- Cut the 9" x 8" piece of coordinating fabric into two strips 2½" x 8" and two strips 1¾" x 8". **Note:** *Scan the QR code for a video on prairie points.*

- Use pins to mark the center of one side of each 2½" wide strip.

- On each 2½" x 8" strip, place a prairie point on each side of the center mark with the wrong side of the prairie points facing the right side of the fabric strip.

Wave Stitch
Needle: Right
Wave/Overlock: Wave
Stitch Width: 7.5 for Wave
Stitch Length: Start with 1.25
Stitch Selector: B
Differential: N
Foot: Utility

- Stitch in place with a ¼" seam using a 4-thread overlock stitch.

- Center a prairie point on the other side of each 2½" x 8" strip and stitch in place.

- Stitch these two strips together matching the single points.

- Complete the square by stitching a 1¾" x 8" strip to the top and bottom of the block.

- Square to 6½".

4-Thread Overlock
Needle: Both
Stitch Width: M
Stitch Length: 2.5 - 3.0
Stitch Selector: A
Differential: N
Foot: Utility

Block Techniques

Ribbon and Lace Block by Betty

Heirloom techniques are quick and easy on your serger. The rolled edge beautifully replaces the sewing machine technique known as 'whip and roll'. This simple block uses the serger rolled edge stitch to attach both the ladder trim and the lace. On this block, the stitches are done with the wrong sides together. This can also be reversed so that the rolled edge stitches show on the surface of the block for a different look.

Supplies

- 7½" square of fabric
- ½ yard of lace insertion
- ¼ yard of ladder trim
- Three spools of serger cone thread

url on page 28

Rolled Edge
Needle: Right Overlock
Wave/Overlock: Overlock
Stitch Width: 3.5
Stitch Length: 1
Stitch Selector: D
Differential Feed: N
Foot: Utility

Construction

- Thread for a 3-thread rolled edge with serger cone thread.

- Cut fabric piece into four equal strips.

- Align the edge of the lace with one cut edge RST.

- Stitch just catching the edge of the lace. Do not cut.

- Stitch the other side of the lace to a second piece of fabric in the same manner.

- Repeat for the other two pieces of fabric.

- The ladder trim will now be used to connect the two pieces of fabric and lace.

- Use the same rolled edge settings and stitching methods to attach the ladder trim in between the two pieces of fabric.

- Weave the ribbon through the ladder.

- Press.

- Square the block to 6½" x 6½".

Note: Scan the above QR code for a video tutorial on how to make the ladder ribbon and lace.

Block Techniques

Ric Rac and Rope Block   by Pam

If you have a cover stitch or chain stitch, your serger is great for applying trims. Whether it is a trim you have purchased or one you have made, adding trim can jazz up any project. The rope (or twisted cord) is made by using decorative threads and twisting them on your bobbin winder.

Supplies for Ric Rac

- Ric rac or desired trims
- Three spools of thread of your choice. (This sample was made with Lamé Stylo thread in the needles.)
- 8" square of fabric
- Double-sided basting tape

Construction

- Set your serger for cover stitch - narrow with thread to match your trim.

- Apply double sided basting tape to the wrong side of your trim or ric rac. Arrange your first trim and stitch it down with your cover stitch.

- Apply each trim as desired.

Cover Stitch - Narrow	
Needle: Center, Right	
Stitch Width: N/A	
Stitch Length: 2.5	
Stitch Selector: N/A	
Differential Feed: 1.0 or N	
Foot: Pintuck or Open Toe	

Supplies for Twisted Cord

- Two spools of thread of your choice to sew on cord
- Twisted cord or four strands of WonderFil™ Razzle™ and/or Dazzle™

Construction

- Cut four cords 2½ times the desired length. Knot together at one end.

- Slide the knotted end through the hole of a bobbin. Place the bobbin on your bobbin winder with the knotted side down and the thread tails up.

- Start your bobbin winder while holding the thread tails tightly. Wind until the thread starts to kink up.

- With your free hand, find the center of the threads, and pull center folding in half so the thread twists into a cord.

- Once you have made your rope trim, use your chain stitch to secure in place.

Chain Stitch - Center	
Needle: Center	
Stitch Width: N/A	
Stitch Length: 2.5	
Stitch Selector: N/A	
Differential Feed: 1.0 or N	
Foot: Pintuck or Open Toe	

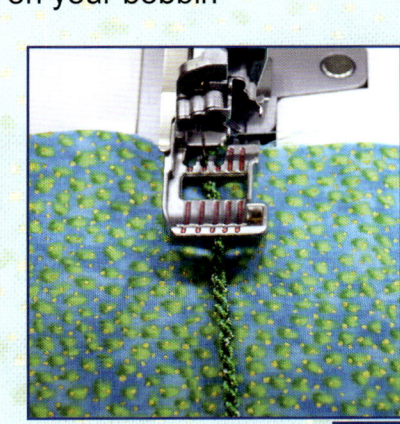

Block Techniques

Ruffles and Waves Block by Betty

This block combines multiple serger techniques. Wave stitch, rolled edge, ruffles, and strip piecing combine to create a colorful block with many more possibilities. Just picture this technique with one or two ruffles on the front of a little girl's dress. Add additional ruffles and create a beautiful pillow. This is a great 'stash' technique and your options are endless!

Supplies

- Center strip 3" x 12" (white on the sample)
- 1st ruffle - one strip 1½" x WOF (yellow)
- 2nd ruffle - one strip 1½" x WOF (green)
- 3rd ruffle - one strip 1½" x 22" (blue)
- Background fabric (pink)
    - One strip - 1" x 25"
    - One strip - 1½" x WOF
    - One strip - 2½" x 10"
- 6½" square ruler or template for shaping the block
- Decorative and serger cone threads
    - Wave stitch - Two coordinating decorative threads and one cone of serger thread. (we used Lamé Stylo)
    - Rolled edges - One decorative thread and two cones of serger thread to match each ruffle. (we used Lamé Stylo) 🧵
    - Gathering and Seaming - Three cones of neutral color serger thread.

url on page 28

Wave Stitch

Needle: Right Overlock
Wave/Overlock: Wave
Stitch Width: 5.0 - 7.5
Stitch Length: 1.0 -2.0
Stitch Selector: B
Differential Feed: N
Foot: Utility
Check that threads are in the correct tension slots for wave.

Construction

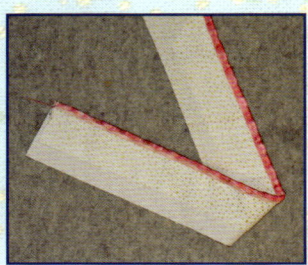

- Fold the center strip over 1" on each long side and press.

- Thread for wave stitch.

- Hold the strip so that you cannot see the wrong side of the fabric. Wave stitch on each fold.

- Press the stitching toward the outside edge.

- Trim excess fabric by setting the ½" line on the inside edge of the stitching. You should have approximately ¼" of your fabric showing.

- Thread the serger for a rolled edge matching the thread for the first ruffle.

Note: Scan the above QR code for a video tutorial on how to make this wave block.

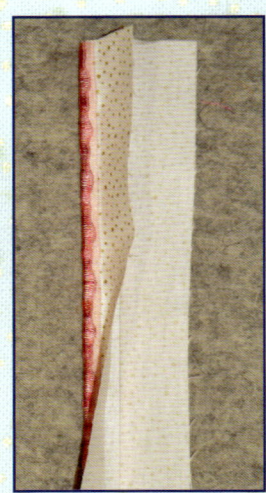

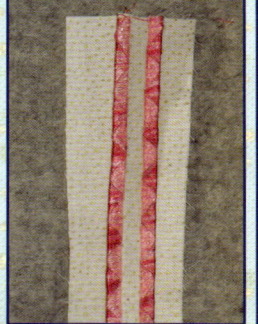
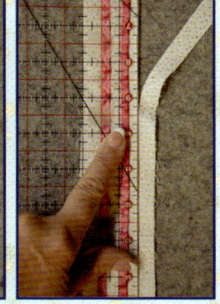

Rolled Edge

Needle: Right Overlock
Wave/Overlock: Overlock
Stitch Width: 3.5
Stitch Length: 1
Stitch Selector: D
Differential Feed: N
Foot: Utility

Ruffles and Waves Block (CONTINUED)

Construction (CONTINUED)

- Stitch the rolled edge on one long side of the strip.

- Re-thread and repeat for the remaining ruffle strips.

- Thread the serger for gathering and attach the ruffling foot. Gathers will be tighter if stitch selector is on D not A.

- Gather the unfinished long edge of each of the rolled edge strips.

- Attach the standard foot and set the serger for a 3-thread overlock - wide stitch.

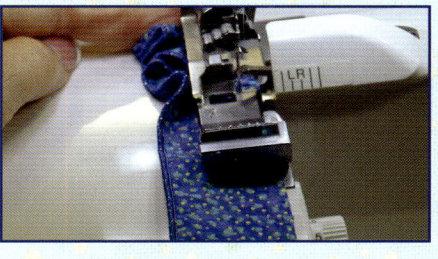

| **Gathering** |
| **3-Thread Overlock - Wide** |
| **Needle:** Left Overlock |
| **Wave/Overlock:** Overlock |
| **Stitch Width:** 6 |
| **Stitch Length:** 3.5 - 4 |
| **Stitch Selector:** D (Yes use D not A) |
| **Differential Feed:** 2 |
| **Foot:** Utility |

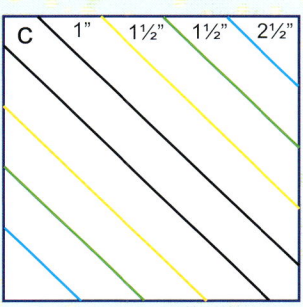

- The diagram on the left represents the background strips. The gold, green and blue lines indicate where the ruffles will be sandwiched between these strips.

- Hold the wave stitching out of the way and stitch the 1" wide background fabric to each side of the center strip.

- Press seams toward the center.

| **3-Thread Overlock - Wide** |
| **Needle:** Left Overlock |
| **Wave/Overlock:** Overlock |
| **Stitch Width:** 6 |
| **Stitch Length:** 2.5 |
| **Stitch Selector:** A |
| **Differential Feed:** N |
| **Foot:** Utility |

- Align the first ruffle with the 1" wide background strip that has been attached to the center strip.

- Stitch.

- Place the 1 ½" wide strip on top, sandwiching the ruffle between the two background strips, and stitch together.

- Repeat for the other side.

- Press toward the center.

- Use the 6½" square ruler to trim corners.

- Attach the second ruffle to the 1½" strip. Sandwich with another 1½" strip. Press and trim the sides.

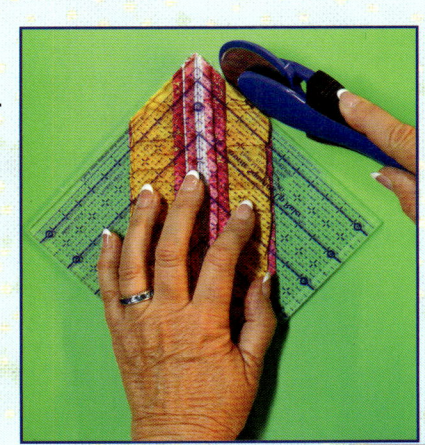

- Attach the third ruffle to this strip.

- Use the 2½" background strip to sandwich the third ruffle.

- Press and use the 6½" square ruler to square the completed block.

Block Techniques

Serger Lace Block by Betty

Serger lace is created with a balanced 3-thread stitch using the left needle and the widest stitch width. Heavy decorative thread is used in the loopers. The weight and colors of the thread do not have to match. Thread in the sample is a combination of WonderFil™ Razzle™ in the upper looper and a coordinating color of Madeira Decora 12 in the lower looper.

Supplies

- 9" x 8" fabric
- One cone serger thread
- One spool WonderFil™ Razzle™ thread
- One spool Madeira Decora 12 thread

url on page 28

Construction

- Depending on the project, the first row of stitching is done either on the raw edge or a folded edge. The stitch length for this row should be short enough to completely cover the fabric. Depending on the thread used, the stitch length will most likely be somewhere between 1.5 and 2.

- Succeeding rows of stitches will just 'bite' into the right edge of the previous row.

- For a narrow ruffle, the stitch length starts at 4 and is decreased by one for each additional row of stitching. (The shorter stitches create fuller ruffles.)

- Thread the serger for a 3-thread overlock - wide stitch.

- Fold the fabric in half across the 8" width and press. (WST)

- Fold again 2 ½" from either side of the center and press. (WST) *Note: Scan the above QR code for a video tutorial on serger lace.*

- Stitch row one on each of these folds.

- Press all three rows in the same direction with the Razzle thread on top. (Pressing now ensures that the lace stays fuller as it tends to flatten out if the folds are pressed after the lace is stitched.)

- Go back to each fold, open flat and add the additional rows of stitching to make the lace. Stitch length of 4 followed by SL 3, SL 2, SL 1.

- Square the fabric to 6 ½", keeping the lace evenly spaced in the square.

3-Thread Overlock - Wide	
Needle:	Left
Stitch Width:	7.5
Stitch Length:	Varies
Stitch Selector:	A
Differential Feed:	N
Foot:	Utility

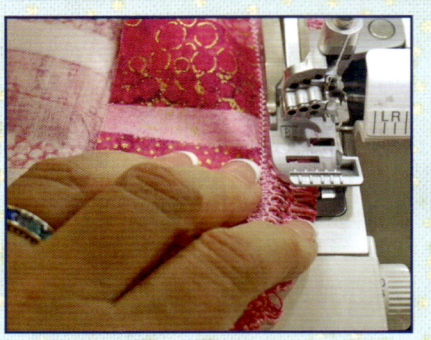

Block Techniques

Stitch and Scrunch Block by Pam

Chain stitch and cover stitch are great ways to add texture and interest to your project. With this "shrinking" product (see supply list below) you can have fun creating dimensional fabric. If your serger doesn't have a cover or chain stitch, use your sewing machine with the decorative thread in the bobbin and bypass the tension. The directions for the shrinking fabric say to allow an additional 15% for shrinking, but we added about 25%.

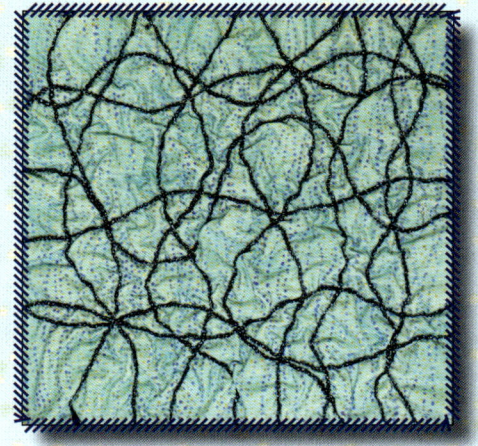

Supplies

- 9" square of fabric
- One cone of serger thread
- Steam iron
- Shrinking fabric (Brand names include Texture Magic™, Heat-N-Shrink® and Krinkle Magic.)
- Decorative thread (we used WonderFil™ Sizzle™.)

url on page 28

Chain Stitch	
Needle: Center	
Stitch Width: N/A	
Stitch Length: 2.5 - 3.0	
Stitch Selector: N/A	
Differential Feed: 1.0 or N	
Foot: Cover/Chain	

Construction

- Place the shrinking fabric on the wrong side of your block of fabric. With your serger set for chain stitch, and the fabric right side down, sew either in a random pattern, in rows or in a grid.

Note: *We used blue painter's tape so you can see how much the fabric will shrink. Scan the above QR code for a video tutorial on how to make this block.*

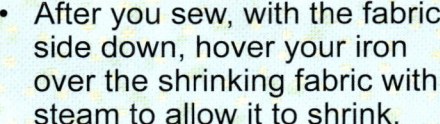

- After you sew, with the fabric side down, hover your iron over the shrinking fabric with steam to allow it to shrink.

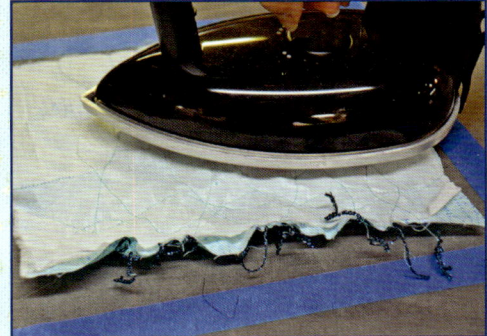

- After the fabric has been shrunk to size, trim to 6½" or to desired size.

Block Techniques

Twisted Tucks Block by Pam

Do you use your serger just to finish seams? Use your 3-thread overlock stitch to create this fun dimensional technique. By simply stitching tucks, folding one row up and one row down, you can create this interesting surface wave finish.

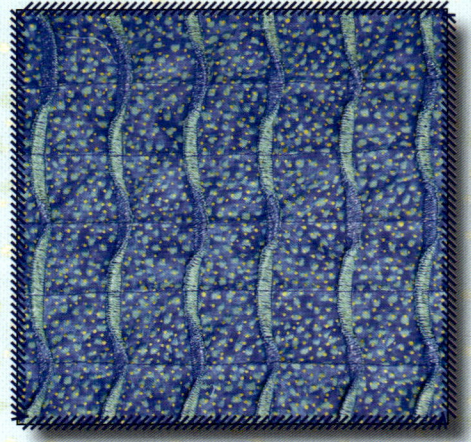

Supplies

- Two spools of decorative thread in coordinating colors (We used Lamé Stylo thread.) 🧵
- Two cones of serger thread
- Fabric cut 7" x 12"
- FriXion® or fabric marking pen 🧵

3-Thread Overlock - Wide	
Needle:	Left
Stitch Width:	6.0
Stitch Length:	1.5
Stitch Selector:	A
Differential Feed:	1.0 or N
Foot:	BL or Open toe foot
Cutter:	Locked

Construction

- Starting at one end, on the right side of the fabric, mark a line 2" from the end.

- Then mark five more lines, each 1½" apart, with the last line 2" from the other end. These will be the fold lines that you will serge on.

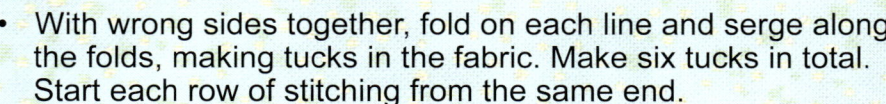

- With wrong sides together, fold on each line and serge along the folds, making tucks in the fabric. Make six tucks in total. Start each row of stitching from the same end.

- Press all tucks down in the same direction.

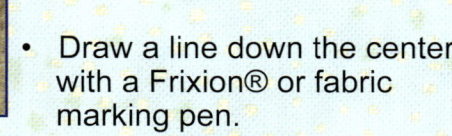

- Draw a line down the center with a Frixion® or fabric marking pen.

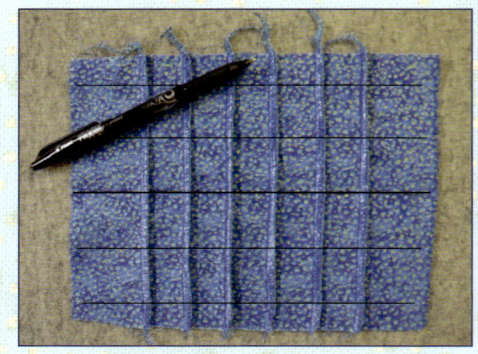

- From the center line, draw two more lines 1" apart for a total of five lines.

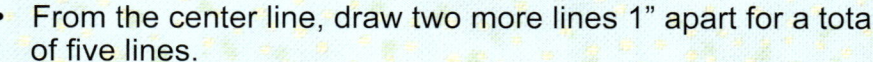

Block Techniques

Construction (CONTINUED)

- Convert the serger to a chain stitch. (If you do not have a chain stitch on your serger, use your regular sewing machine for this step.) Thread with regular cone serger thread.

Chain Stitch	
Needle:	Center
Stitch Width:	N/A
Stitch Length:	3
Stitch Selector:	N/A
Differential Feed:	1.0 or N
Foot:	Chain/Cover Stitch

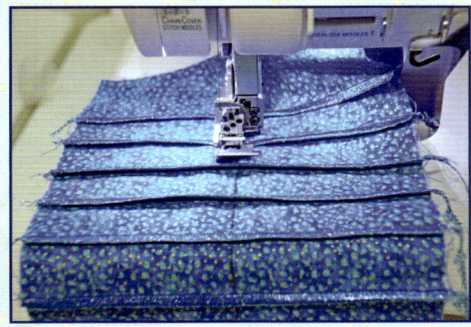

- With the right side up, sew down the center, securing pleats in the same direction.

- Turn the fabric around and stitch the next two lines that are each 1" from the center in the opposite direction.

- Turn the fabric around again and stitch down the two outer lines in the opposite direction of the lines you just stitched.

- Press the block flat, pressing the ends in the opposite direction from the last row of stitching, so one tuck goes up and the next goes down, and so on.

- Trim the block to 6½" and serge the remaining ends to fold back one more time.

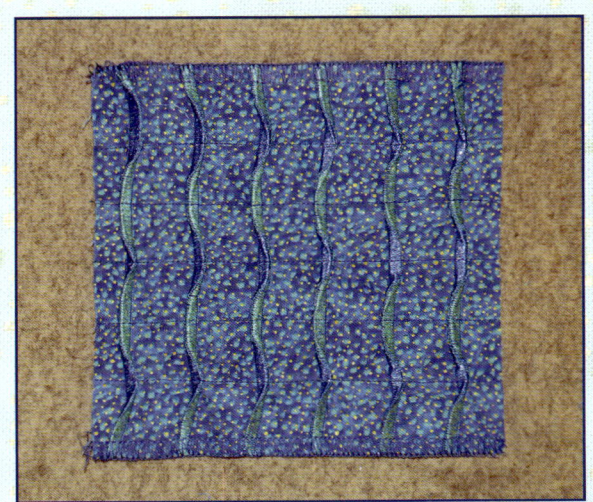

Digital Download Page

Scan this QR code or enter the following url into an internet address bar to get a digital copy of this page of product and video tutorial links!

Beaded Rolled Edge (page 30) https://www.youtube.com/watch?v=JQM5WKbb8gw&feature=youtu.be

Beaded Serger Necklace (page 102) https://www.youtube.com/watch?v=NREQdo_Gia8&feature=youtu.be

Belt Loop Trim (page 32) https://www.youtube.com/watch?v=gGMj1dGyHy4&feature=youtu.be

Betty's Serger Quilt, quilting (page 84) https://www.youtube.com/watch?v=HEPCeAPLhXs&feature=youtu.be

Betty's Serger Quilt, wave piping border (page 83) https://www.youtube.com/watch?v=qp7E7atHz-s&feature=youtu.be

Box Pleated Trim (page 37) https://www.youtube.com/watch?v=4IgCvoSo8yc&feature=youtu.be

Decorative Trim Block, double piping (page 16) https://www.youtube.com/watch?v=yHzrbSh4McI&feature=youtu.be

Evening Bag, piping (page 61) https://www.youtube.com/watch?v=STSlmnOVU_M&feature=youtu.be

Evening Bag, ruffle (page 62) https://www.youtube.com/watch?v=irzqsXjbKgg&feature=youtu.be

Heirloom Pillowcase, rolled edge pintucks (page 90) https://www.youtube.com/watch?v=n--nveDxzio&feature=youtu.be

Knife Pleated Trim (page 37) https://www.youtube.com/watch?v=igrmxjjeFIM&feature=youtu.be

Mini Wonder Wallet (page 44) https://vimeo.com/231016913/32b677dde7

Pintuck Block (page 18) https://www.youtube.com/watch?v=Zn1hEyt7Es8&feature=youtu.be

Prairie Points Block (page 19) https://www.youtube.com/watch?v=jPRj5iw28Ic&feature=youtu.be

Purslet® (page 48) https://vimeo.com/231016913/32b677dde7

Ribbon and Lace Block (page 20) https://www.youtube.com/watch?v=0_JnqX7giXY&feature=youtu.be

Ruching (page 40) https://www.youtube.com/watch?v=_LoDAku1IEM&feature=youtu.be

Ruffled Jeans (page 98) https://www.youtube.com/watch?v=xFkpURkyrfs&feature=youtu.be

Ruffled Towel (page 101) https://www.youtube.com/watch?v=N6dUM4jBxRw&feature=youtu.be

Ruffles and Waves Block (page 22) https://www.youtube.com/watch?v=utee0vxe7VE&feature=youtu.be

Ultimate Pillow Template (page 96): https://www.youtube.com/watch?v=TiLvoFvaYMg&t=132s

Serge Protector, folded ribbon (page 67) https://www.youtube.com/watch?v=1Xnx2xRwK84&feature=youtu.be

Serger Lace Block (page 24) https://www.youtube.com/watch?v=As9c4m9NuAc&feature=youtu.be

Serger Headband, flower design (page 104) https://www.dropbox.com/s/buphtk5nuot5rvv/Daisy.zip?dl=

Stitch and Scrunch Block, fabric scrunching (page 25) https://www.youtube.com/watch?v=nxfsrYO0zbs&feature=youtu.be

Wave Stitch Piping (page 41) https://www.youtube.com/watch?v=pgOjnFGpbB0&feature=youtu.be

Zipper Insertion (page 42) https://www.youtube.com/watch?v=fXtZxJ4N_nw&feature=youtu.be

Zipper Genie (page 42): https://www.youtube.com/watch?v=recp3cX2Db4

Great Finishes

Beaded Rolled Edge Ruffle by Pam

This is a trim taught to me by Betty. It's a great eye catching finish and your friends will wonder how it's done!

Supplies

- 6 pound nylon fishing line
- Beads
- Box Pleat Tape® by Pam Damour
- Ruffle fabric, cut on the bias and folded in half with wrong sides together, and cut to desired length (two to three times full).
- Three spools of serger thread, or two spools of serger and one spool of heavy decorative thread.
- Cover chain foot (optional)

url on page 28

3-Thread Rolled Edge
Needle: Right
Stitch Width: medium (normal)
Stitch Length: 1.5 - 2.0
Stitch Selector: D
Differential: Normal
Foot: Cover Chain

Construction

- Set your serger up for a 3-thread rolled edge. If using a heavy thread, put it in the upper looper.

- Place the box pleat tape ¾" from the folded fabric edge. If you don't have the tape, you'll need to mark out where to insert the beads.

- Calculate how many beads you will need and string them onto your fishing line.

- Begin by serging a few inches of rolled edge along the folded edge of the ruffle.

- Then, starting with about 4" of fishing line and with 2" sticking out, serge about 2" of rolled edge with the fishing line encased.

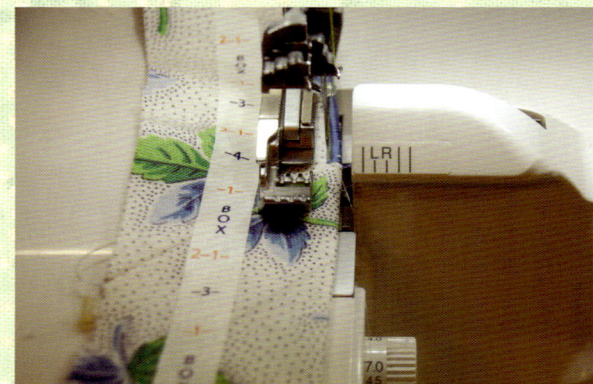

- You will need to hold the line to the right of the needle.

- Stop when the foot is even with a -1- on the tape. Make a loop with the fishing line, with a bead in the loop.

Note: Scan the above QR code for a video tutorial on how to make beaded rolled edge.

Great Finishes

Construction (CONTINUED)

- Serge to the next -1-. Pull the excess slack out of the line so the bead is snug to the stitching.

- Repeat until your trim is complete.

- To splice the ruffle, leave about 2" at each end without the rolled edge. Overlap the ends as shown and serge the seam.

- Press seam open and flat and press fold.

- Serge the remaining edge and add beads by hand if necessary.

- Gather to size with your ruffler, or use a box pleat to make cluster pleats at the corners of our sample.

Great Finishes

Belt Loop Trim by Pam

In addition to making the basket weave block on page 10, your belt loop binder attachment can make belt loops, trims, straps, and ties. Here's a great trim you can make!

Supplies

- Belt loop binder: either ¾" or 1½"
- Utility foot or curve foot
- Strips of fabric cut SLIGHTLY wider than the shovel on your bias binder. *For example:* For the small binder cut ⅞"; for the large binder cut 1⅝".
- You will need about 8 times your finished width for 2" trim.
- Water-soluble stabilizer
- Thin ruler or yardstick to wrap the belt loop tape around.
- Wonder Clips®

url on page 28

Cover Stitch – Wide	
Needle: Right, Left	
Differential Feed: 1.0 or N	
Stitch Width: N/A, Cutter locked	
Stitch Length: 3.0	
Stitch Selector: N/A	
Foot: Curve or Utility	

Construction

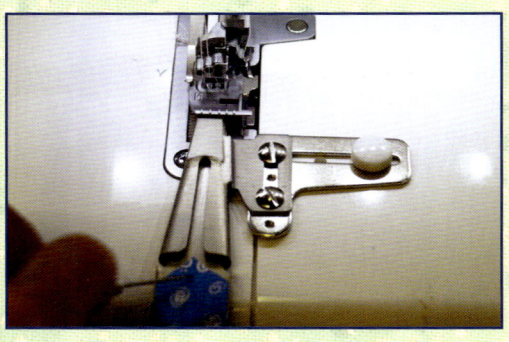

Note: Scan the above QR code for a video tutorial on how to make belt loop trim.

- Set the serger for wide cover stitch

- To start, cut your fabric to a point.

- Use a stiletto to guide the fabric into the binder.

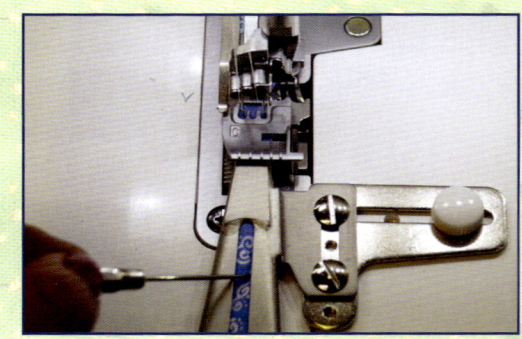

- Bring the fabric under the foot, past the needle, and begin serging.

- When you need to insert a second piece of fabric strip, allow it to slightly overlap the fabric already in the binder.

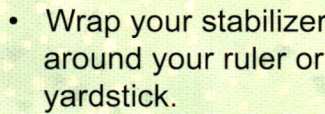

- The overlap of two pieces joined is shown here.

- Wrap your stabilizer around your ruler or yardstick.

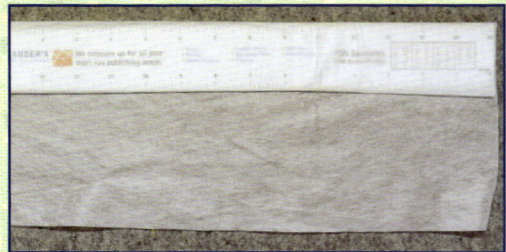

Great Finishes

Belt Loop Trim (CONTINUED)

- Secure the end of the belt loop trim to the ruler with a Wonder Clip®. Wrap trim around the ruler. Be sure not to wrap too tightly so you can slide everything off the ruler.

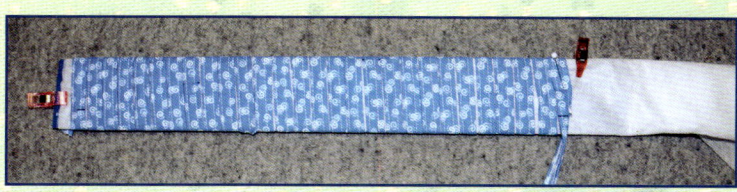

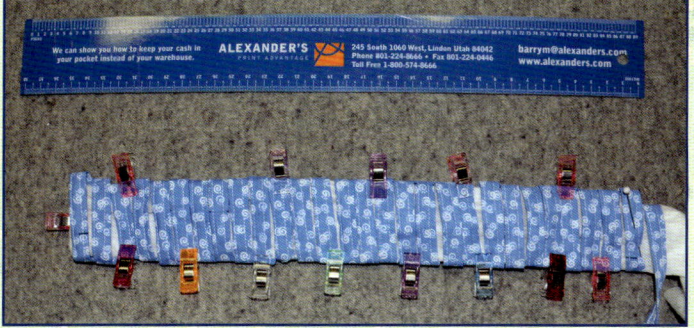

- After you have wrapped enough trim for your project, slide it all off the ruler. Hold the wraps in place with Wonder Clips®.

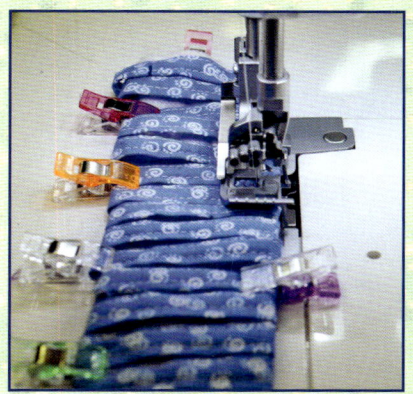

- Convert your serger to chain stitch and stitch along one edge to secure the loops.

- Soak the trim in water to remove the water-soluble stabilizer.

- Press the trim flat and sew it into project.

Chain Stitch
Needle: Center
Stitch Width: N/A
Stitch Length: 3
Stitch Selector: N/A
Differential Feed: 1.0 or N
Foot: Chain/Cover Stitch

Covered Elastic by Pam

There are times when we need elastic in a project, such as the Sewing Caddy on page 58 or the Headband on page 104. Making your own custom embellished elastic is easy using any serger.

Supplies
- ¼" elastic to cover
- One spool of WonderFil™ Razzle™
- One spool of WonderFil™ Spaghetti™
- One spool of matching sewing or serger thread

Construction
- With your serger set up for a 3-thread overlock - wide, serge over the elastic, trimming off the excess. Always test your stitch first to make sure your settings are right for your thread and elastic. You may have to lengthen or shorten your stitch to create a satin stitch. The thread should completely cover the elastic.

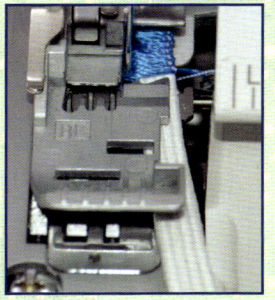

3-Thread Overlock – Wide
Needle: Left
Differential Feed: N
Stitch Width: 6.0
Stitch Length: 2.0
Stitch Selector: A
Foot: Curve

Great Finishes

Continuous bias is a term that refers to the technique where fabric is sewn into a tube, then cut in a spiral fashion to create bias strips in a very fast and efficient manner. It requires no more fabric than cutting straight grain strips of fabric.

• Begin with a square or rectangle of fabric. We are showing a rectangle as most of the time your fabric will be rectangular. Remember that a square is just a rectangle with four equal sides.

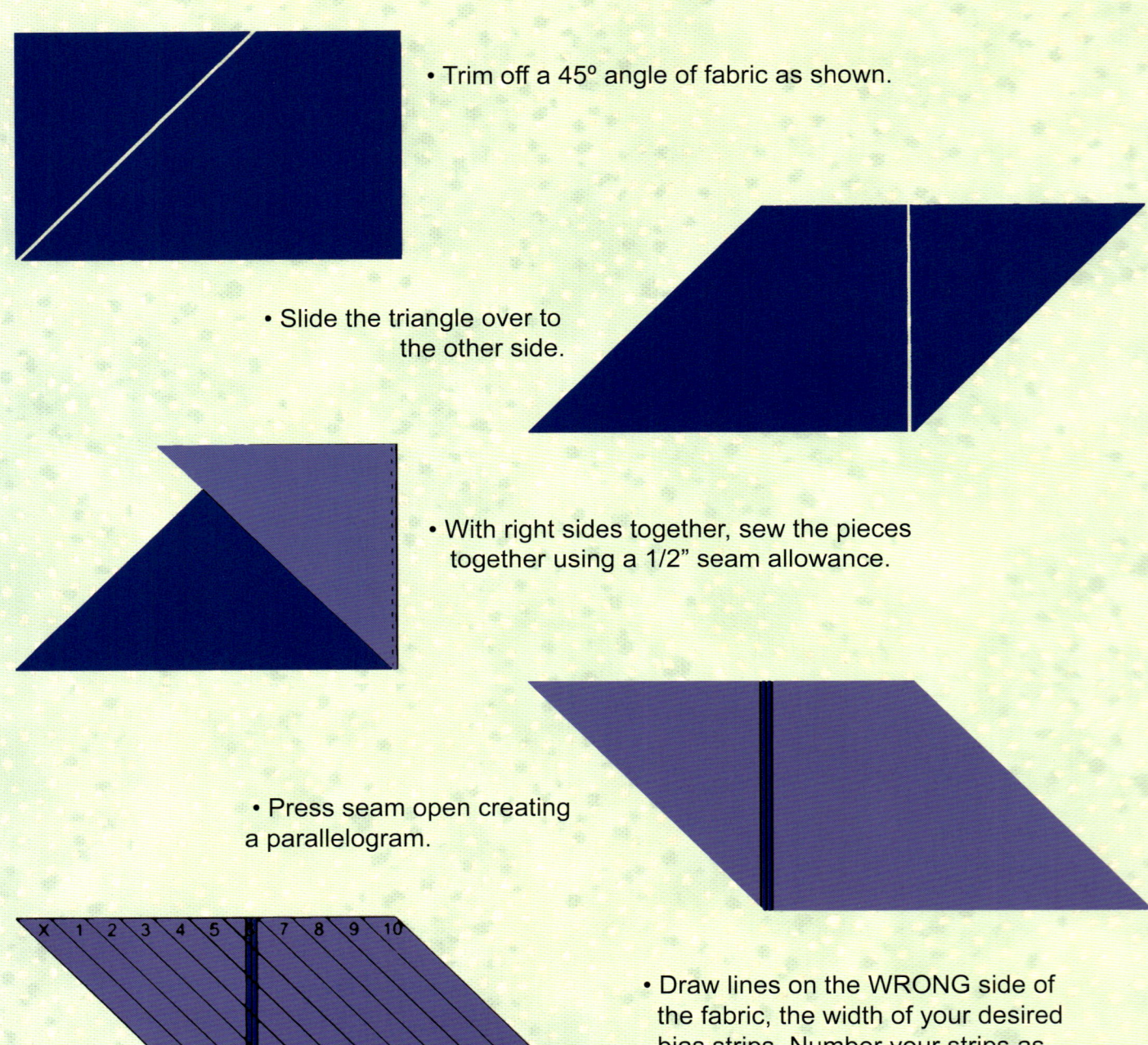

• Trim off a 45° angle of fabric as shown.

• Slide the triangle over to the other side.

• With right sides together, sew the pieces together using a 1/2" seam allowance.

• Press seam open creating a parallelogram.

• Draw lines on the WRONG side of the fabric, the width of your desired bias strips. Number your strips as shown.

Great Finishes

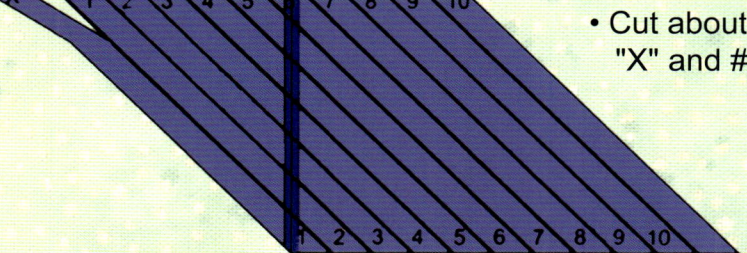

• Cut about 2" on the line between the "X" and #1.

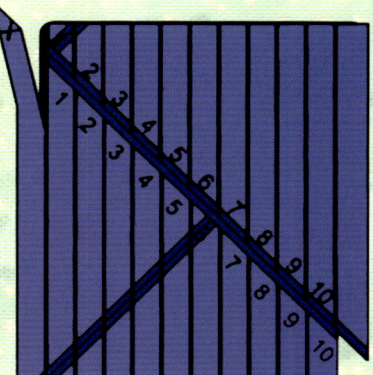

• Line up the numbered strips so the same numbers are together. With right sides together, pin, making sure like numbered strips are aligned and stitch a ½" seam. Press all seams open and flat. Cut on the drawn lines to create easy, uniform bias strips.

 This bias can be used for single welt cord, double welt cord, ruffles, ruching, shirred welting, bias binding, and banding.

MATH FORMULAS FOR CALCULATING CONTINUOUS BIAS

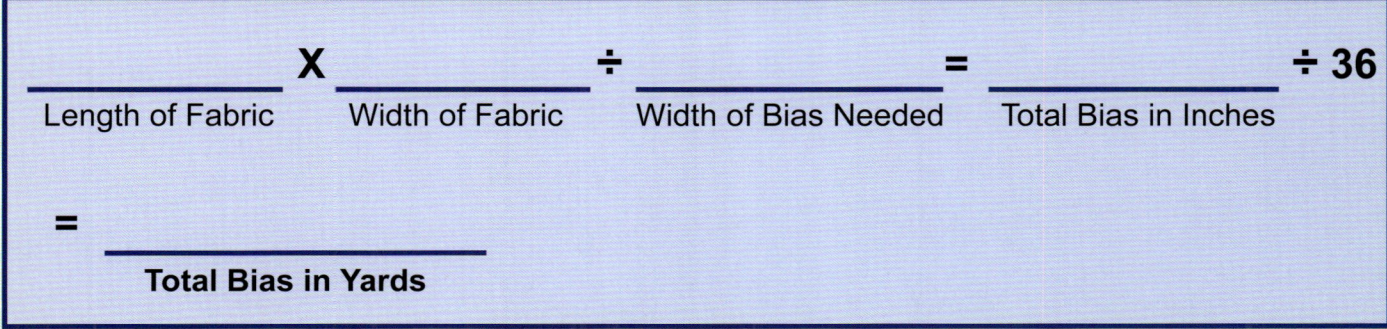

_____ X _____ ÷ _____ = _____ ÷ 36
Length of Bias   Width of Bias   Width of Material   Amount of Inches

= _____
Amount in Yards

OR If you have a piece of fabric and want to know how much bias it will yield:

_____ X _____ ÷ _____ = _____ ÷ 36
Length of Fabric   Width of Fabric   Width of Bias Needed   Total Bias in Inches

= _____
Total Bias in Yards

Great Finishes

Piping by Pam

Piping can be easily made with a serger. You can also use a serger to attach ready-made piping. Use a piping or cording foot with a groove in the bottom to hold the cord in place.

Supplies
- Micro Welt Cord® 🪡 or Standard Welt Cord® 🪡
- 2" wide bias-cut fabric strips
- Hemostats

3-Thread Overlock - Wide
Stitch Width: 7.5
Stitch Length: 3.0
Stitch Selector: A
Differential: 1.0 or N
Foot: Cording/Piping

Construction

- Attach the piping foot. With the bias fabric folded over the cord and raw edges to the right, line up the cord with the groove in the bottom of the foot.

- Once your piping is made, you can serge the piping to the right side of the fabric.

- When you get close to the corner, clip the seam allowance ½" from the corner, clipping all the way to the cord.

- Stitch all the way off the corner. Clip the seam allowance all the way to the cord where you need to turn the corner, bend the cord corner and place the project back under the foot.

Joining Piping

- To join the piping, allow about 1½" to 2" of overlap.

- Pull an inch of cord out of the piping with hemostats and cut it off.

- Do the same thing at the other piping end.

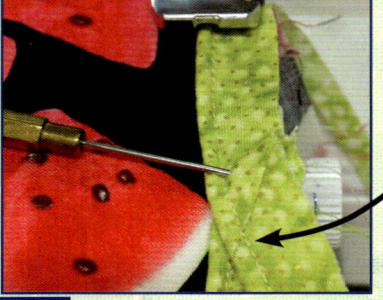

- Overlap as shown.

- Serge across the overlap.

36

Great Finishes

Pleated Trims and Inserts by Pam

Box Pleats

Box pleated trim and inserts are a cinch with the Box Pleat Tape by Pam Damour. You can make box pleats 1", 2", 3" and 4". The best part is this tape is reusable!

url on page 28

Supplies

- Box Pleat Tape® by Pam Damour
- Brass stiletto
- Three cones of serger thread
- Fabric to be pleated, cut three times the finished length

3-Thread Overlock - Wide

Stitch Width: 6.0
Stitch Length: 3.0
Stitch Selector: A
Differential: 1.0 or N
Foot: Curve or Clear

Construction

- Thread the serger for a 3-thread overlock - wide.

- Place the tape on your fabric and line up the numbers following the directions on the packaging.

- Use a stiletto to hold the pleats in place as you serge. When making box pleats, the folds should meet at the top and bottom of each pleat.

- Allow 3X fullness for each pleat technique, regardless of the size or type of pleat.

Helpful Hint: When pleating your fabric, make the pleat before your fabric is under the foot. As you begin to serge a pleat under the foot, pleat up to the next fold. Scan the above QR code for a video tutorial on how to make box pleats.

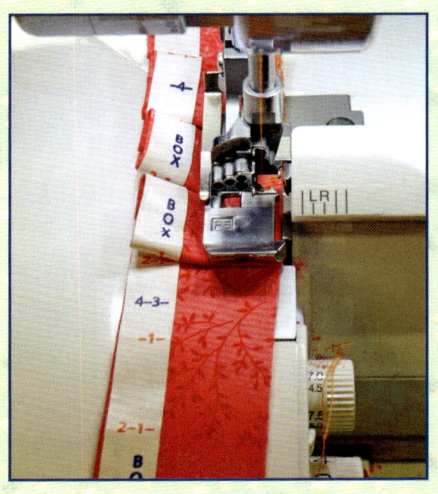

Knife Pleats

Knife pleated trim and inserts are fast and easy with Knife Pleat Tape by Pam Damour. Use them as an insert or an edge trim. Place the tape on your fabric and line up the numbers following the directions on the packaging. You can make knife pleats 1", 2", and 3" and, like the box pleat tape, it is reusable.

Note: Scan this QR code for a video tutorial on how to make knife pleats.

url on page 28

Great Finishes

Pleated Trims and Inserts (CONTINUED)

Knife Pleats (CONTINUED)
Supplies
- Knife Pleat Tape® by Pam Damour ✻
- Brass stiletto ✻
- Fabric to be pleated cut three times the finished length
- Three cones of serger thread

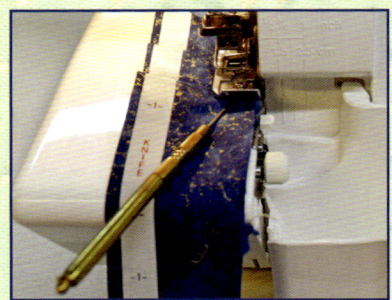

Construction
- Thread the serger for a 3-thread wide overlock.

- Use a stiletto to hold the pleats in place as you serge.

- When making knife pleats, the bottom fold will end where the top fold starts.

- Allow 3X fullness for each pleat technique, regardless of the size or type of pleat.

Pleated Windows

When making pleated windows, the fabric needs to be cut on the bias. Allow three times fullness. The settings are the same for knife or box pleated windows. On box pleated window, the pleats will be folded back in both directions. (See page 12.)

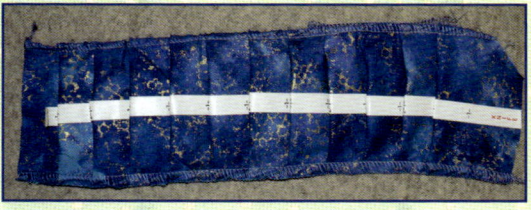

- Pleat the fabric, following the box or knife pleat directions on the previous page.

- Stitch both edges down, barely trimming off any fabric.

- Remove the tape.

3-Thread Overlock - Wide
Stitch Width: 6.0
Stitch Length: 3.0
Stitch Selector: A
Differential: 1.0 or N
Foot: Curve or Clear

- Fold each pleat back in the opposite direction and hold in place with your stiletto as you sew with a chain stitch.

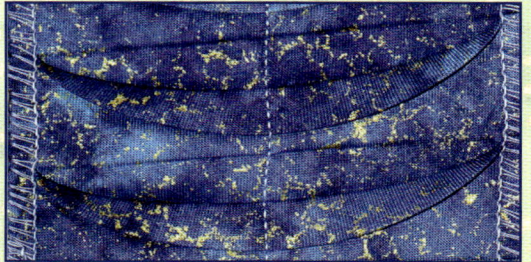

Note: to see a video of pleated windows, use the QR code for the knife pleat trim video and watch to the end!

Great Finishes

Rolled Edge Piping by Pam

Piping can be easily made with a serger. You can also use a serger to attach readymade piping. Use a piping foot with a groove in the bottom to hold the cord in place.

Supplies

- One spool or cone of WonderFil™ Razzle™ or Dazzle™ or other eight-weight thread
- Two cones of matching serger thread
- 1½" wide bias fabric
- 5-in-1 Ruler® by Pam Damour

3-Thread Wide Rolled Edge

Needle: Left
Stitch Width: 3.5
Stitch Length: 1.25
Stitch Selector: D
Differential: 1.0 or N
Foot: Utility Foot

Construction

- Set up your serger for a 3-thread wide rolled edge, with your needle in the left (wide) position.

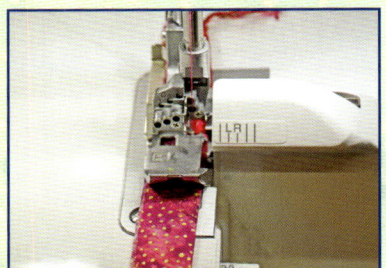

- Thread the upper looper with the eight-weight decorative thread.

- Fold your bias-cut fabric in half with wrong sides together.

- Serge along the folded edge.

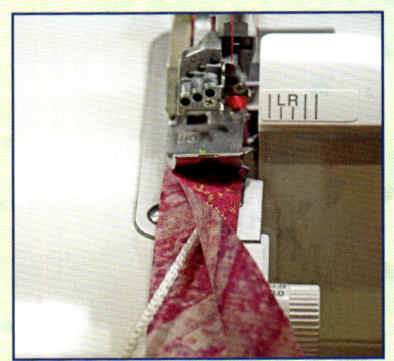

- To make a more raised rolled edge piping, add Micro Welt Cord® and follow the above instructions. Trim with the 5-in-1 Ruler®.

3-Thread Overlock - Wide

Stitch Width: 7.5
Stitch Length: 3.0
Stitch Selector: A
Differential: 1.0 or N
Foot: Cording/Piping

- Use your cording foot to serge this piping onto a project.

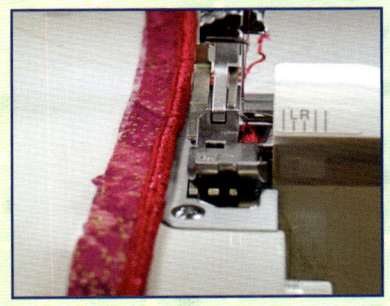

- Join the ends by overlapping as you would for the wave stitch piping. (See page 36.)

Great Finishes

Ruffles and Ruching by Pam

Ruffles are easy to make with the serger. Single layer light weight fabrics work best. Ruching is when the ruffle is gathered on both sides. It's the perfect insert for your sewing project, shown here in the center of this pillow

Supplies

- Ruffle or gathering foot
- Three or four spools of thread of your choice.
- Fabric cut three times the finished length, preferably on the bias

url on page 28

3-Thread Overlock - Wide

Needle: Left
Stitch Width: 7.0
Stitch Length: 4.0
Stitch Selector: D
Differential: 2.0
Foot: Ruffle or Gathering

Construction

- Examine your ruffler before attaching it to the serger. If the bottom flange does not have a gap like the one shown, gently pull it out to look like this. (See photo on left.)

- Run your fabric through using a ⅜" seam allowance.

- Keep your left index finger behind the heel of the foot to help the fabric gather. Now you have a ruffle!

- To make ruching, gather on one side, then gather the other side the same way. Your finished ruching should be about 3X full. *For example,* for each foot of ruching, you will need three feet of flat fabric.

Note: Scan the above QR code for a video tutorial on how to make ruching.

Great Finishes

Wave Piping Trim by Pam

If you have a serger with the wave stitch, try this easy trim. You can create the wave stitch right on the project or make it a trim that can be added to your project.

Supplies

- 1½" wide bias strip of fabric
- One spool of serger thread
- 5-in-1 Ruler® by Pam Damour
- Two spools of decorative thread (I used a 12 weight.)

url on page 28

Construction

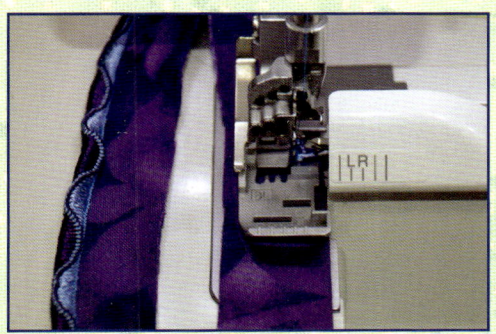

- Set up the serger for wave stitch; drop the cutter.
- Fold and press the fabric in half lengthwise, wrong sides together.
- Serge along the folded edge with the fold against the right edge of the foot as shown.

3-Thread Wave Stitch

Needle: Left
Wave Stitch: Wave
Stitch Width: 7.0
Stitch Length: 1.5
Stitch Selector: B
Differential: 1.0 or N (normal)
Foot: Utility Foot
Cutter: Locked

Caution: Because the cutter is locked, it is important that you keep the folded edge even with the edge of the foot to avoid damage to your looper.

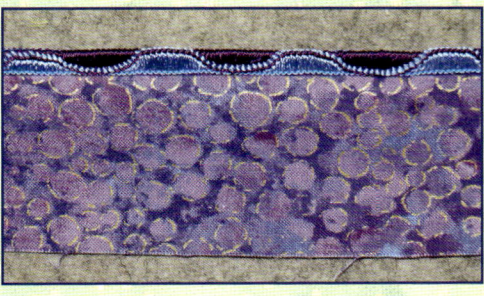

- After your trim is stitched, use the 5-in-1 Ruler® to trim any seam allowance in excess of ½".
- To serge wave stitch piping onto your project, use the settings on the right.

3-Thread Overlock - Wide

Needle: Left
Stitch Width: 7.0
Stitch Length: 2.5
Stitch Selector: B
Differential: 1.0 or N
Foot: Cording/Piping

- Insert the trim onto the edge of the project, stitching along the edge of the wave stitch piping.
- Serge the piping into place.
- Join it by overlapping ends.

Note: Scan the above QR code for a video tutorial on how to make wave stitch piping.

Great Finishes

Zipper Insertion by Pam

Zippers are fun to put in with the serger. When Using a piping foot, the groove in the foot will hold the zipper teeth in place.

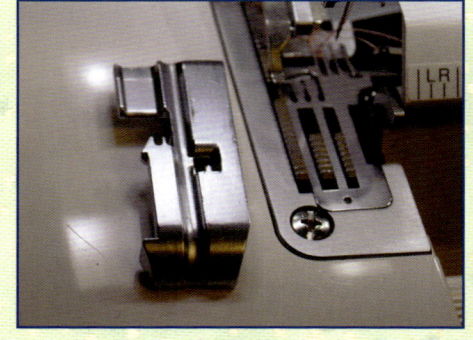

Supplies
- Cording or piping foot
- Zipper tape by the yard
- Zipper slide
- Optional: Zipper Genie®

url on page 28

Construction
- Separate the zipper into two sections.

- Treat each zipper section like piping. (Because, hey! That's what it looks like!)

- Serge one side of the zipper to each piece of fabric.

- Using the end of the zipper slide with the two holes, insert each section of the zipper tape into the holes. This is done one side at a time, angling each side in toward the slide. Once each side is barely catching, push the back of the slide down until you feel the clicking of the zipper.

- Zip the slide all the way off the end of the zipper.

- Reinsert the slide as you did earlier, leaving the slide in the center of the zipper of your project.

Note: Scan the above QR code for a video tutorial on zipper insertion.

Are you having trouble getting your slide on your zipper?
We have a great tool called the Zipper Genie®.

This tool can hold your slide in place as you insert both sides of the zipper teeth creating an easy insertion! For more information, go to the link on page 28, or scan this QR code.

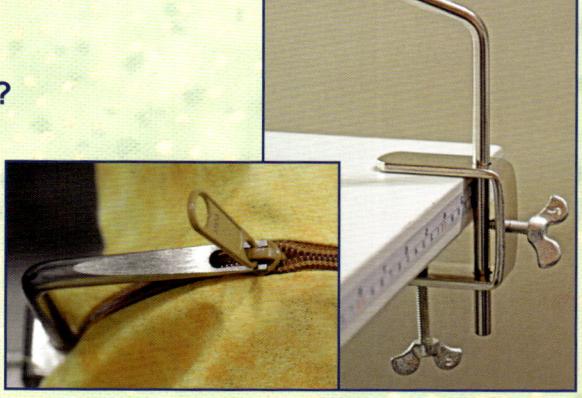

url on page 28

Clutches
and Covers

The Mini Wonder Wallet   by Pam

The Mini Wonder Wallet uses the small (4⅜") wallet clasp by Pam Damour. You can make in 90 minutes! It has four card pockets, a currency pocket and a zippered pocket. Since this is made on the serger, all top stitching is done by chain stitch. If your serger doesn't have a chain stitch, you can use your sewing machine.

Supplies

- Wallet outside: cut one 13" x 7½"
- Wallet lining: cut one 14¾" x 7½"
- Accent pocket: cut one 4" x 7½"
- Pocket Peel & Stick Stabilizer®
    Cut one 4¼" x 7½" for the zipper pocket
    Cut three 2" x 7½" for the card pockets
    Cut one 3" x 7½" for the currency pocket.
- Single Side Super Shaping Foam®, cut one 4¼" x 7½"
- 7½" zipper tape and one slide
- Small 4⅜" wallet clasp
- Glue gun
- Basting tape
- Size 00 Phillips Head Screwdriver

url on page 28

Construction

- Prepare your wallet pieces for construction by adding stabilizers.

Outer Fabric

- To the wrong side, stick the zipper pocket stabilizer piece on one end.

- Fuse the foam, leaving ⅛" gap between the foam and the pocket stabilizer.

- Stick 2" pocket stabilizer, leaving a ⅛" gap between the stabilizer and foam.

Pocket Assembly

- On the wrong side of the lining, stick 3" stabilizer on the end of the wallet lining. This will create your currency (top) pocket.

Chain Stitch - Center
Needle: Center
Stitch Width: N/A
Stitch Length: 2.5
Stitch Selector: N/A
Differential Feed: 1.0 or N
Foot: Cover/Chain

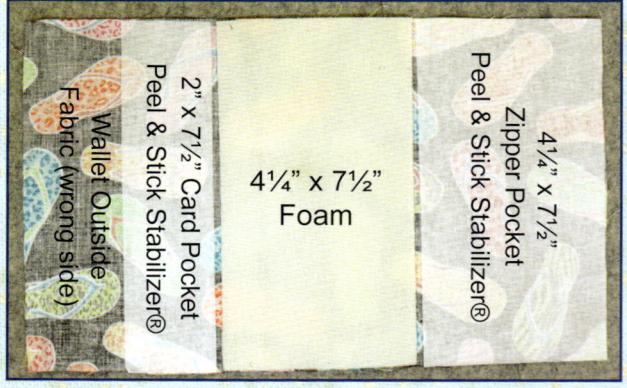

Wallet Outside Fabric (wrong side) | 2" x 7½" Card Pocket Peel & Stick Stabilizer® | 4¼" x 7½" Foam | 4¼" x 7½" Zipper Pocket Peel & Stick Stabilizer®

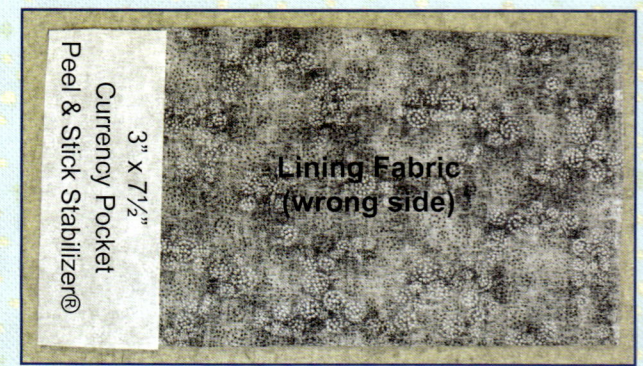

3" x 7½" Currency Pocket Peel & Stick Stabilizer® | Lining Fabric (wrong side)

Clutches and Covers

Construction (CONTINUED)

Accent pocket

- Stick the 2" pocket stabilizer on the wrong side of the pocket.

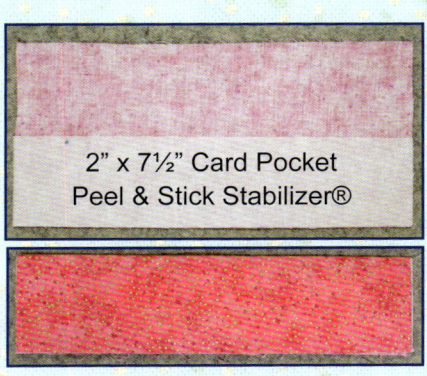

2" x 7½" Card Pocket
Peel & Stick Stabilizer®

- Fold the pocket in half lengthwise with wrong sides together and press.

- Chain stitch ⅛" from the folded edge.

Zipper Pocket Insertion

3 ½"

- On the wrong side of the outside fabric where you have fused the Pocket Peel & Stick Stabilizer®, draw a zipper box. This box is 6" long, ½" wide, and is 3½" from the end (see photo). (See page 49 for more info.)

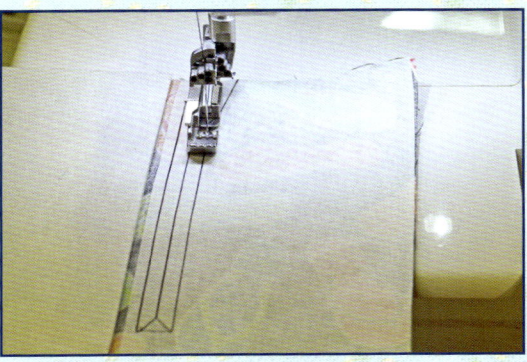

- Chain stitch all the way around the box, starting and stopping along a long side.

- Cut down the center and snip the "Y" at the ends all the way to the corners, being careful not to cut into the stitching.

- Pull the lining through the opening and press flat. Place the zipper on the back side, centered in the opening, right side up. Add basting tape to keep it from shifting.

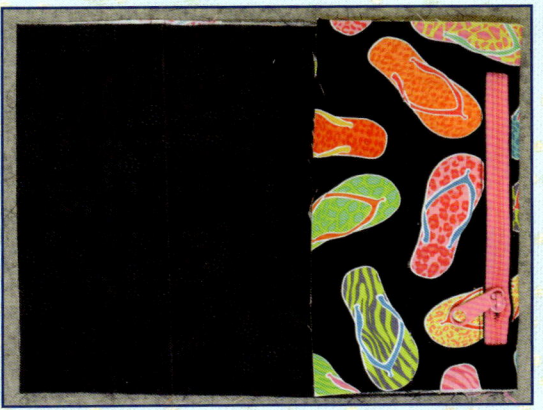

- Chain stitch along the edge of the opening, again starting along a long edge. For more complete instructions on the zipper insertion, refer to page 49.

- The last step in zipper insertion is to fold the wallet over ¼" from the top so the edge of the wallet is even with the edge of the foam, approximately 4¼" from top.

Mini Wonder Wallet (CONTINUED)

Construction (CONTINUED)

Pocket Assembly

- Fold the other end of the wallet outside up 2", with wrong sides together. Press on the fold and top stitch ⅛" from the folded edge.

- On the opposite end of the zipper pocket, with wrong sides together, fold the lining over 2" along the edge of the stabilizer.

Fold to here

- Press a crease on this fold and top stitch ⅛" from the folded edge.

- Arrange the card pocket (pink) on top of the currency pocket. Allow approximately ½" spacing.

- Stitch the bottom of the accent pocket (pink) onto the lining of the currency pocket.

- Stitch along this folded edge and fold up to make the third row of pockets.

- Mark a line up the center of the card pockets. Starting at the bottom, stitch along one side of the line. When you get to the top edge of the second pocket, stop and pivot 90°.

- Stitch one stitch across the line, again pivot 90°, then stitch back down to the bottom of the pockets on the other side of the line.

Construction (CONTINUED)

Finishing

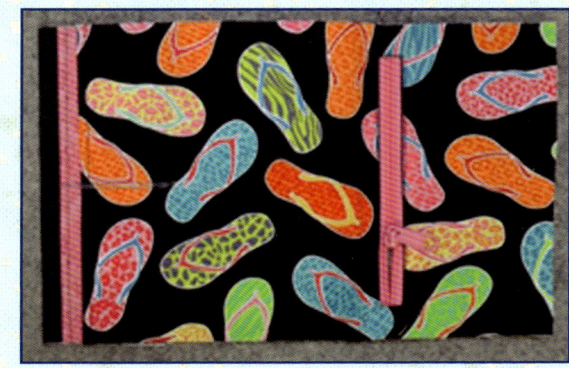

- Fold the wallet and double check to make sure it will fit into your clasp. (You may need to adjust your fold line to fit the clasp properly.)

- Serge across each end to hold all layers in place.

- On one end, snip into the stitching to allow for the clasp opening.

- Remove the inner layers so that the outer layers can be tucked into the center.

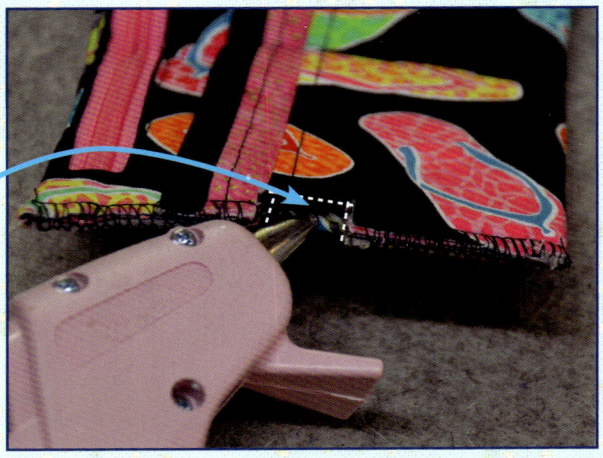

- Using a glue gun, put a small amount in the tuck to hold everything in place. (See page 52.)

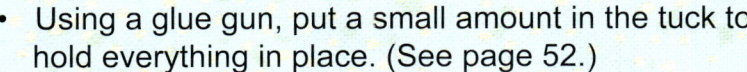

- Heat your clasps with an iron. Once your clasps are hot, add a small amount of hot glue inside each end.

- Slide each end of the fabric into the clasps, with the screw holes to the inside. Allow the glue to set. Install screws in each side until they are flush with the frame. They may not screw tightly so feel free to secure them with a small amount of glue.

The Purslet® by Pam

The Purslet® is more than a wallet. It has six pockets for cards, two currency pockets and a large zippered pocket. In addition, there is an outside pocket for your cell phone and there are two tabs with D-rings for a chain strap. This is all made on your serger.

Note: If your serger doesn't have a chain stitch, you will want to use your sewing machine for some of the steps.

Supplies

- Wallet outside: cut one 8½" x 27"
- Zipper pocket: cut one 8½" x 8½"
- Currency Pocket: cut one 8½" x 6½"
- Card pockets: cut three 8½" x 4"
- Outside pocket: cut one 8½' x 8½"
- Strap tabs: cut two 3" x 2"
- Single Sided Super Shaping Foam® 🪐
  Cut one 8½" x 7½", and one 7½" x 1½"
- Pocket Peel & Stick Stabilizer® 🪐
  Cut one 7½" x 3¼", and three 7½" x 2"
- 7½" Quick Clutch Wallet Clasp® 🪐
- 48" bag chain with D-rings 🪐
- 7½" zipper with slide 🪐
- Basting tape 🪐
- Glue gun and glue stick
- FriXion® or fabric marking pen 🪐
- Wonder Clip® by Pam Damour

url on page 28

Chain Stitch
Needle: Center
Stitch Width: N/A
Stitch Length: 2.5
Stitch Selector: N/A
Differential Feed: 1.0 or N
Foot: Utility or Chain

8½" x 7½"
Foam

Construction

- Place the end of the larger piece of the Super Shaping Foam® flush with one end of the wrong side of your outside fabric and fuse with ½" of fabric extending on each side.

- Quilt if desired, but know that with the Super Shaping Foam® quilting is not necessary.

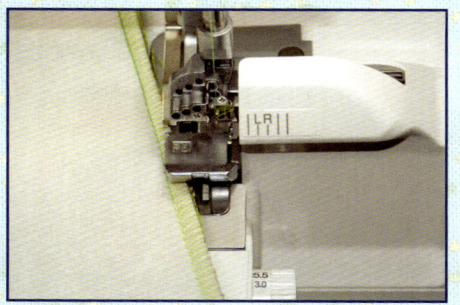

- With right sides together, serge the outside pocket to the padded end allowing ¼" seam allowance. (See serger settings.)

- Roll the fabric around the end to make it look like piping. Stitch in the ditch using your chain stitch.

- On the opposite end of the outside pocket fabric, fuse the smaller piece of Super Shaping Foam® to the wrong side flush with the end, leaving a ½" seam allowance on each side.

Clutches and Covers

Construction (CONTINUED)

Pocket Assembly

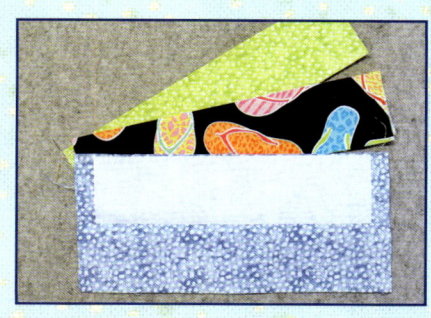

- Fold all three card pocket sections and currency pocket section in half lengthwise, with wrong sides together.

- Place the Pocket Peel & Stick Stabilizer® in each pocket section, up to the folded center, with ½" seam allowance on each end.

- Chain stitch along the folded edge of each section and arrange the three card pockets on top of the currency pocket. Allow approximately ½" between each row.

- Starting with the top card pocket, chain stitch along the bottom edge of each pocket, sewing ¼" from the bottom edge. Repeat with the middle and bottom pockets.

- Mark a line up the center. Chain stitch along one side of the line, starting from the bottom.

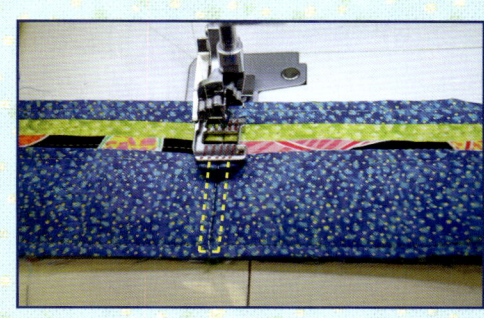

- When you get to the top edge of the third pocket, stop and pivot. Chain stitch one stitch across the line and stitch back down to the bottom of the pockets, on the other side of the line.

Zipper Pocket

- Fold your zipper pocket lining in half, with wrong sides together. Press to put a sharp center crease. On the wrong side of the fabric, draw a zipper box with a FriXion® or fabric marking pen. Position it ½" below the center crease, 6½" long and ½" wide.

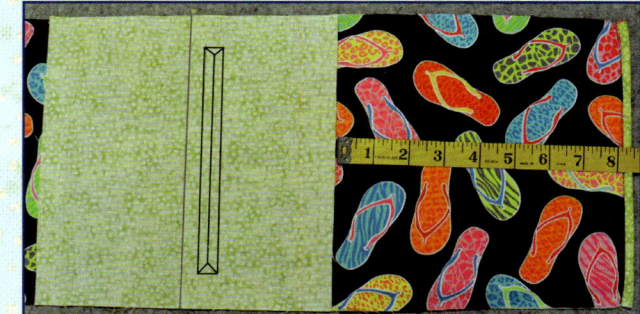

- Down the center of the box, draw a line, making a "Y" at each end.

- With right sides together, place the zipper pocket lining with pocket edge 8½" from the edge of the padded edge.

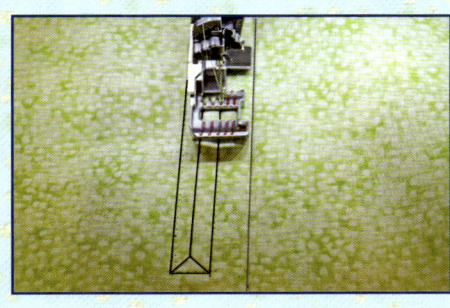

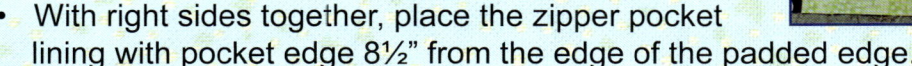

- Starting in the middle of one of the long sides, chain stitch carefully on your zipper box line, pivoting at each corner.

- Cut down the center of your box, cutting to each corner.

Clutches and Covers

Purslet® (CONTINUED)

Zipper Pocket (CONTINUED)

- Prepare your zipper by inserting the slide. Put the basting tape on the right side, with the basting tape near the outer edges of the zipper.

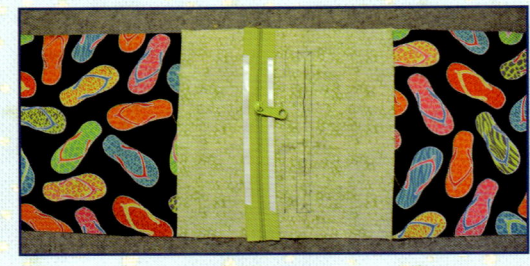

- Pull the lining fabric through the opening and press flat.

- Center the zipper teeth under the opening. Chain stitch along the edge of opening.

- Trim off the zipper tape at the ends so that it does not get stitched in the outer seams.

- With right sides of the outer pocket together, pin or Wonder Clip® the outer pocket to the quilted end of the outer fabric, 1" from edge.

- Baste the edges to keep it from shifting.

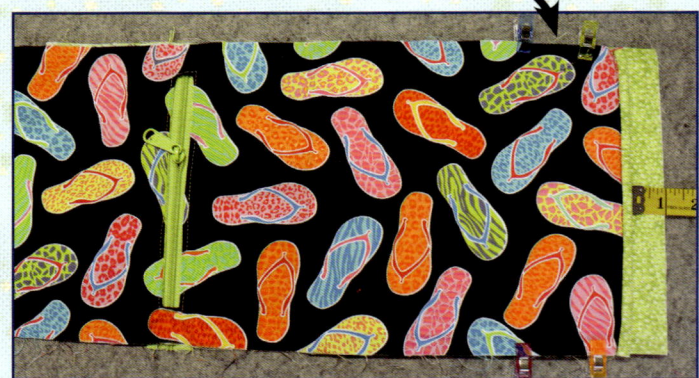

Pocket Placement

- On the wallet inside end, place the pocket assembly 1" from the top edge.

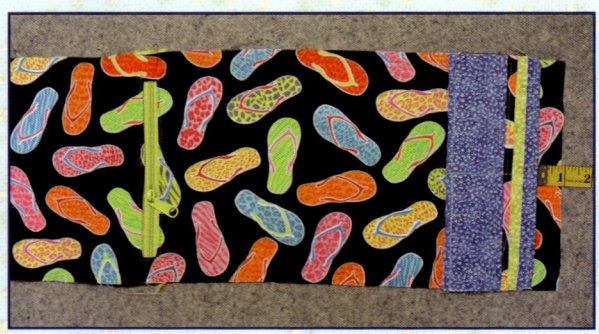

- Wonder Clip® or pin in place.

- Sew along the bottom edge of the pockets with a ¼" seam allowance.

Purslet® (CONTINUED)

Pocket Placement (CONTINUED)

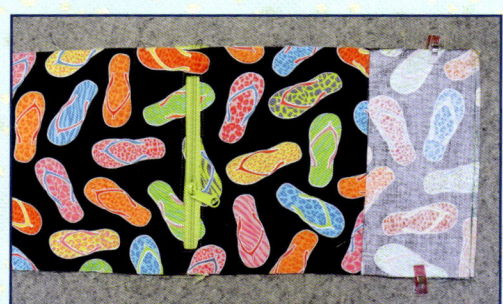

- Fold the wallet fabric over the bottom edge of the pockets, RST.

- Chain stitch along the previous stitching line.

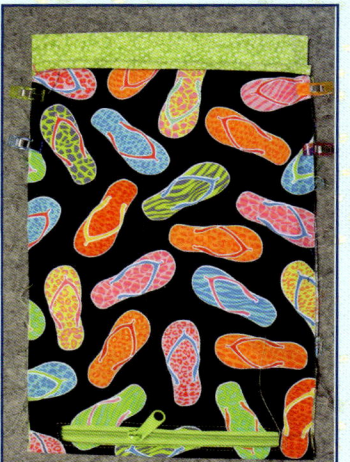

- Fold the wallet over ½" from the zipper opening and line up the two ends of the outer fabric. The outside should look like this.

- The inside of the wallet should look like this before the zipper pocket is folded up.

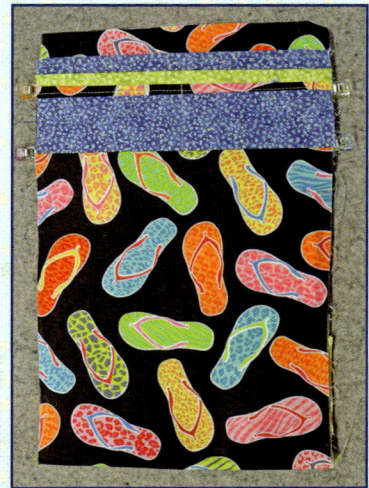

- Fold the zipper pocket up so the inside looks like this.

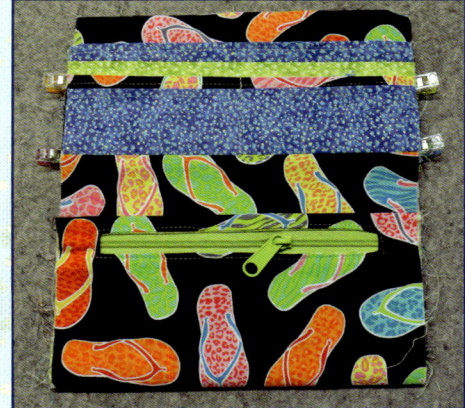

- Pin or Wonder Clip® the zipper pocket to the wallet lining for stability.

- Reverse fold the wallet at the bottom edge so right sides are together and serge along each side. Turn right sides out and press flat.

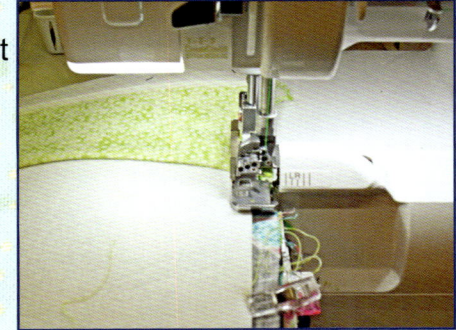

- Stitch along the edge of the foam.

- Turn right side out and press flat.

Clutches and Covers

Purslet® (CONTINUED)

Construction (CONTINUED)

Strap Tabs

- Make strap tabs by folding raw edges inside, like double fold bias tape.

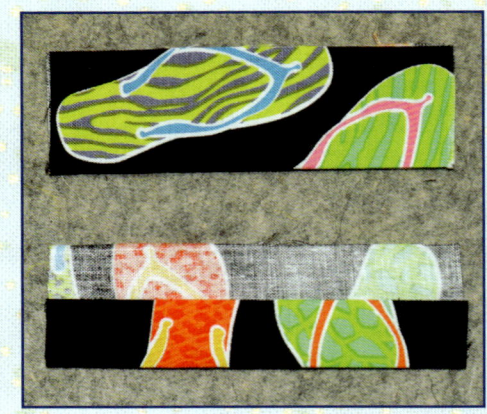

- Chain stitch along the folded edges. Fold tabs in half, with the D-ring in the fold.

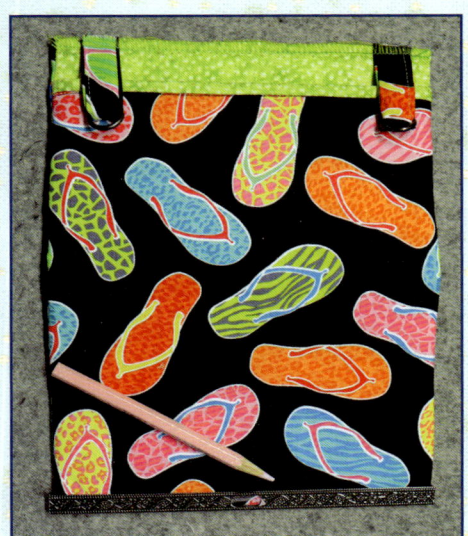

- Pin each tab ½" from the side edge of the wallet. Serge in place with a ¼" seam allowance. Serge the top edge of the wallet to secure all the layers

- On the bottom edge, mark where the clasp hole is to indicate where you need to cut away the fabric. Snip into the bottom edge about ½" and cut away the inner layers. Fold the two outer layers into the center and secure with hot glue.

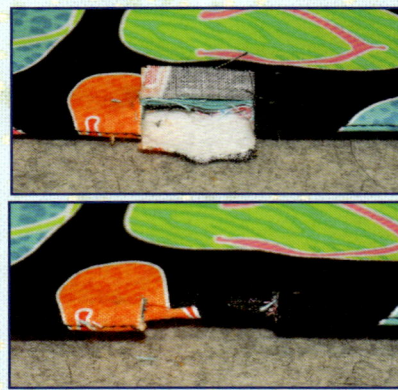

- Heat your clasp with the iron. Once it is hot, add a small amount of hot glue inside at each end.

- Slide the clasp onto each end with the screw holes facing in, allow the glue to set. Install screws in each side until flush with the frame. They may not screw tightly so feel free to secure them with a small amount of glue.

Note: If the screw holes are too small, we use a small flathead screwdriver to stretch the hole enough for the screw.

Need help?

Scan the QR code at the beginning of this project to see a video tutorial on how the Wonder Wallets go together, or use the url address on page 28.

Laptop Sleeve by Betty

This sleeve is the perfect way to protect your laptop or tablet. The attached pocket makes all those cords easy to find and store as well. Due to the size of the pieces to be quilted, this project works great when quilted on the Ovation or Triumph.

Supplies

- ⅝ yard outside fabric for the front and back
- ⅝ yard lining fabric for the front and back
- Two pieces of fabric 7" x 9" each for the pocket
- One yard zipper tape and two slides 🪡
- Basting tape 🪡
- Four cones of serger thread for quilting and seaming
- Small package of Double Side Fusible Super Shaping Foam® 🪡
- Two spools of decorative thread in colors to coordinate with your fabric
- Quilting bar for your serger or sewing machine
- 7 Corner Ruler® by the Sew Sisters 🪡
- FriXion® pen or Magic Fabric Crayon® for marking 🪡

Construction

Calculate size of front and back
- To determine the amount of fabric to cut you will first need to measure the vertical and the horizontal circumference of your laptop.

- Add 5" to each measurement.

- Divide each by 2.
  This will give you the size of the fabric to cut and quilt for the front and the back of the cover.
      Example: Vertical = 22" + 5" = 27½" = 13½".
                  Horizontal = 32" + 5" = 37½" = 18½".
                  Therefore, cut the front and back 18½" x 13½" each.

- Cut pieces of Double Side Super Shaping Foam® to match the front and back pieces of the outside fabric.

Fusing the Shaping Foam
- Sandwich the Double Side Super Shaping Foam® between the outside fabric and the lining fabric for both the front and back pieces of the cover.

- Cut a 5" x 7" piece of Double Side Super Shaping Foam® and center it on the wrong side of one pocket piece. Place the other pocket piece on top and fuse together (make a sandwich).

Laptop Sleeve (CONTINUED)

Construction (CONTINUED)

Quilting and Serging

Chain Stitch Center
Needle: Center
Wave/Overlock: NA
Stitch Width: NA
Stitch Length: 2.5
Stitch Selector: NA
Differential: N
Foot: Chain/Cover
Attach Sewing Table

- Mark diagonal perpendicular quilting lines on the front and back pieces. (The quilting lines on the 7 Corner Ruler® and Magic Fabric Crayon® were used for the samples. You may want to use a FriXion® Pen on lighter color fabrics.)

- Thread the serger for a center needle chain stitch using matching or coordinating thread.

- Attach a quilting bar and a cover chain stitch foot to your serger at the widest point possible. If your serger or sewing machine does not have a quilting bar, mark all of your quilting lines.

- Stitch on the two marked quilting lines.

- Continue quilting by aligning the quilting bar with the previous rows of stitching.

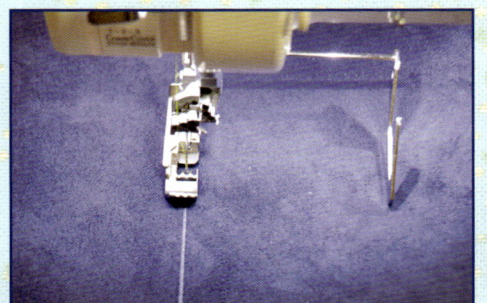 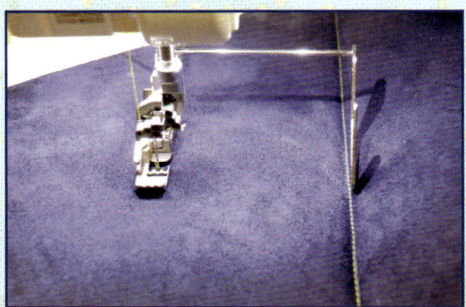 

NOTE: Quilting bar works just as well when placed on the left side of the needle if there is too much fabric on the right side.

- Once you are finished quilting, you will need to square the front and back pieces.

- The finished size should be one inch smaller in both length and width than the pre-quilted pieces. (example: If you first cut your pieces 18½" x 13½", you will square to a finished size of 17½" x 12½".)

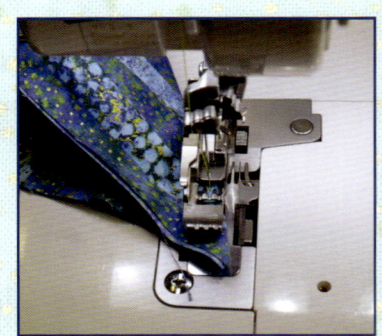

- Prepare the pocket: On the back side of the pocket piece, fold two adjoining sides onto each other at one corner.

- Using a chain stitch, begin stitching where you can just feel the corner of the Super Shaping Foam® that is fused in-between the two pieces of fabric. Stitch a narrow tuck at the corner. Repeat for the other three corners of the pocket.

Laptop Sleeve (CONTINUED)

Quilting and Serging (CONTINUED)

- Use the ½" curve on the 7 Corner Ruler® to slightly trim each corner.

- To prepare for the zipper, cut the pocket into two pieces. On the 9" width cut a 2" wide strip off of the top edge.

- Using your coordinating decorative threads, thread the serger for the wave stitch.

NOTE: In order to make the wave stitch more pronounced we used the left needle position rather than the right and set the stitch selector on A rather than B.

Wave Stitch

Needle: Left Overlock
Wave/Overlock: Wave
Stitch Width: 7.5
Stitch Length: 1-2
Stitch Selector: A*
Differential: N
Foot: Utility
Check that threads are in the correct tension slots for Wave.
*This setting will give you a wider wave.

- Wave stitch on the edges created when you cut the pocket into two pieces.

- Wave stitch on one long edge of both the bag front and bag back.

- Cut a piece of zipper tape 9" long.

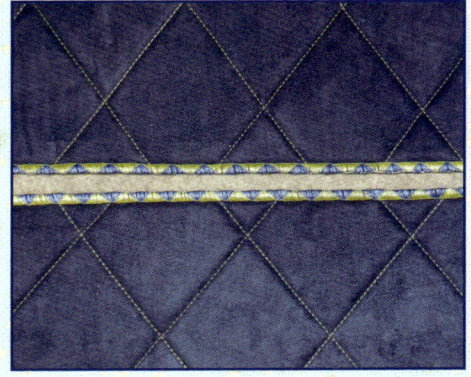

- Place basting tape on the right sides of the zipper tape.

- Tape a pocket piece to each side of the zipper, keeping the edge of the wave stitching close to the zipper teeth.

- Attach a zipper slide to the pocket zipper, see page 42 for details.

- While the serger is still threaded for wave stitch, stitch around the outside edge of the pocket, turning at the corners. To stitch around the curves, keep your fingers to the left of the presser foot and next to the needles. Use a twisting pressure to stitch the curve. It may be necessary to stitch a little, lift the foot and turn the fabric and then stitch some more until you have completed the curve.

Laptop Sleeve (CONTINUED)

Construction (CONTINUED)

- Cut a piece of zipper tape to match the long edge of the laptop sleeve front.

- Apply basting tape to the zipper tape as you did for the pocket zipper.

- Tape the zipper to the front and back pieces of the cover along the wave stitched edges.

- Thread the serger for a right needle chain stitch and attach the cover chain stitch foot.

Chain Stitch Right	
Needle:	Right
Wave/Overlock:	NA
Stitch Width:	NA
Stitch Length:	2.5
Stitch Selector:	NA
Differential:	N
Foot:	Cover Chain

- For the pocket pieces and the front and back pieces of the sleeve, align the right edge of the foot with the right edge of the wave stitching and stitch one side of the zipper in place. For the pocket, it will be necessary to move the zipper slide out of the way as you stitch. For the sleeve, it will be easier if the zipper is separated into two pieces.

- Repeat for the other side of the zipper.

- Insert slide on zipper two times (See page 42 for more details.)

- Apply basting tape to the inside of the pocket as shown.

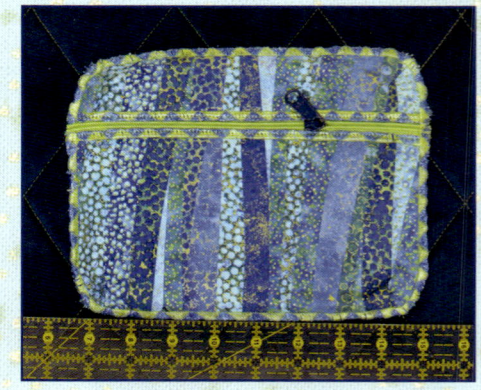

- Center the pocket on the outside of the front 2" from the bottom edge using the basting tape to hold it in place.

Laptop Sleeve (CONTINUED)

Construction (CONTINUED)

- Attach cover/chain stitch foot. Chain stitch in place close to the outside edge of the wave stitching.

- Stitch again just to the left of the wave stitching. This will look like a cover stitch on the outside of the pocket. The two rows of chain stitching were chosen because the curves at the corners are a little easier than with cover stitch and I wanted to 'bury' the inside stitch into the edge of the wave. The width of your wave stitch will vary depending on the thickness of the thread you selected.

- See page 42 to put the bag front and back zipper back together and then to attach the slide.

- Thread the serger for a 4 - thread overlock stitch and attach a utility foot.

- With the laptop sleeve inside out stitch each side from the zipper down securing the beginning by encasing the 'chain tail' in the stitching.

- Stitch across the bottom edge. Secure the beginning by encasing the chain.

- Secure the end by turning the corner at the end and stitching over the stitches on the side for 1"- 2".

- Turn right side out!

4 - Thread Overlock
Needle: Left and Right Overlock
Wave/Overlock: Overlock
Stitch Width: 6
Stitch Length: 2.5
Stitch Selector: A
Differential: N
Foot: Utility

Clutches and Covers

Sewing Caddy by Pam

This easy project goes together in a snap. It's the perfect size to hold sewing supplies, make up, a first aid kit, and more!

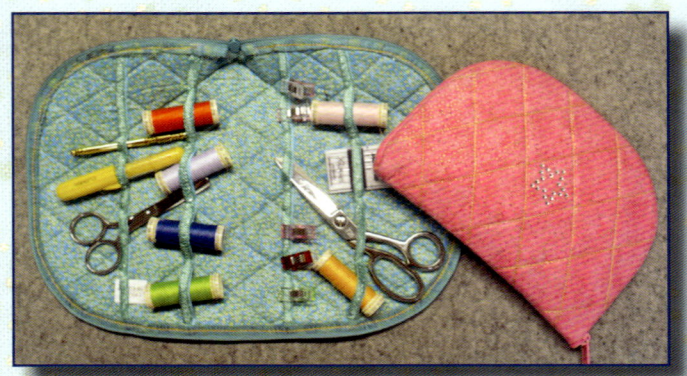

Supplies

- One fat quarter
- 9" x 13" Double Side Super Shaping Foam®
- 1¼ yard of zipper tape and one slide (You will only use one side of the zipper, so save the other side for your next project!)
- Matching or decorative thread
- Serger thread
- One yard of ¼" elastic (see page 33 for covered elastic)
- 7 Corner Ruler® by the Sew Sisters
- FriXion® pen

Chain Stitch - Center	
Needle:	Center
Wave/Overlock:	NA
Stitch Width:	NA
Stitch Length:	2.5
Stitch Selector:	NA
Differential:	N
Foot:	Cover/Chain

Construction

- Using the 3" corner on the 7 Corner Ruler®, trim each corner of the Super Shaping Foam® to create an oval.

- Cut two rectangles 10" x 14" from the fat quarter.

- With wrong sides together, fuse the two rectangles to the Super Shaping Foam, sandwiching the foam in the middle.

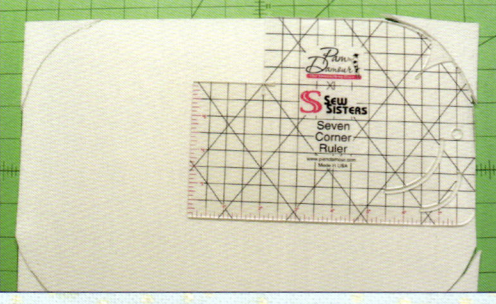

- Trim the fabric, cutting it ½" larger than the foam all around.

- Mark a line across the center with a FriXion® pen.

- Draw parallel lines 1½" out from each side of the center. Draw two more lines 2" out from these lines.

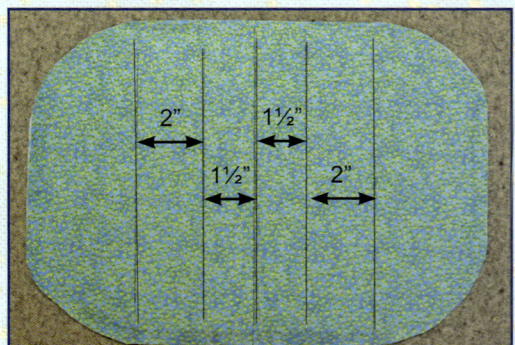

- Draw diagonal quilting lines, using the grid on the 7 Corner Ruler®.

- Using the parallel lines as a guide, pin or wonder clip two or three rows of ¼" elastic on each side of the center line. If you choose to use covered elastic, see page 33. Quilting will hold these in place.

Sewing Caddy (CONTINUED)

Construction (CONTINUED)

- Quilt as desired, using a chain stitch on the serger, or with a regular sewing machine.

3-Thread Overlock - Wide	
Needle: Left	
Stitch Width: 7.5	
Stitch Length: 3.0	
Stitch Selector: A	
Differential: 1.0 or N (normal)	
Foot: Cording/Piping	

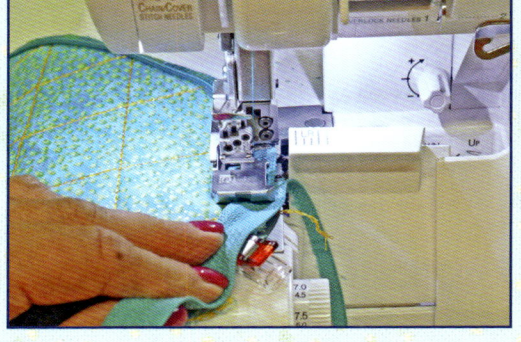

- Using a cording foot on the serger with the width set at 7.5, place the zipper teeth under the piping groove and trim off the excess zipper lip.

- Starting in the center, with 2" of zipper end extended, place the zipper teeth down and serge all the way around, leaving 2" of zipper tape at the end. The free ends of the zipper will overlap by 2".

  Note: *A 2" excess at each end is essential*

- Fit a zipper slide onto the ends of the zipper tape and slide up to where it is sewn to the bag.

- Insert the zipper slide, with the pull through the opening to look like this.

- Pull the zipper end out as shown and serge across the end of the zipper to secure it.

- Press seam allowances toward the inside and top stitch with your sewing machine, or a chain stitch on the serger.

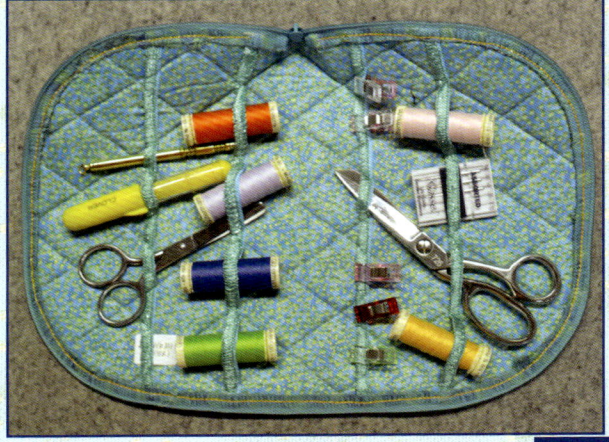

Elegant Evening Bag by Betty

This lovely little bag combines several of the techniques found in the technique blocks. Pintucks embellish the fabric while ruffles adorn the top and do not forget the piping that helps with the structure of the bag!

Supplies

- 9" x 18" piece of satin fabric for the outside
- 7" x 13" piece of satin fabric for the lining
- 7" x 13" piece of batting
- 1½" x 20" piece of satin, cut on the bias to cover cord
- 20" Micro Welt Cord®
- Magnetic bag clasp
- YLI Wooly Nylon thread to match the organza
- Four spools of serger cone thread to match the satin fabric.
- Quilting guide
- Two pieces of organza for the ruffle, one 2" x 60" and one 2" x 20"
- Double Stick Tape® by Pam Damour
- FriXion® pen
- ¾ yard of ¼" twisted cord (or make your own, see page 21)
- Fantastic Fusible Fabric Backing®
- Stiletto

Cover Stitch - Right Narrow
Needles: Center, Right
Stitch Width: N/A
Stitch Length: 2.5 - 3.0
Stitch Selector: N/A
Differential: N (normal)
Foot: Pintuck
Attach Sewing Table.

Construction

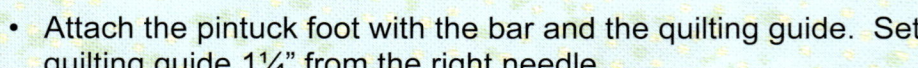

- Thread the serger for cover stitch - right narrow.

- Attach the pintuck foot with the bar and the quilting guide. Set the quilting guide 1¼" from the right needle.

- Stitch tucks on the crosswise grain of the 9" x 18" piece of fabric using the guide to space the tucks.

- Press tucks in one direction.

- Stitch tucks on the lengthwise grain of the fabric using the quilting guide and stitching so that you are securing the pressed folds on the crosswise tucks. Do not press the lengthwise tucks.

- Thread the serger for a 3-thread rolled edge stitch using cone thread in the needle and lower looper and Wooly Nylon thread in the upper looper. Serge one long side of the organza strip with a 3-thread rolled edge stitch.

- Join the short edges of the organza strips with a 3-thread rolled edge stitch.

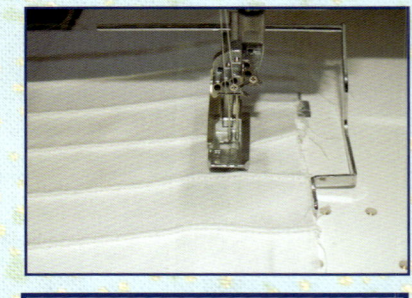

3-Thread Rolled Edge
Needles: Right
Wave/Overlock: Overlock
Stitch Width: M
Stitch Length: 1R
Stitch Selector: D
Differential: N (normal)
Foot: Utility

Elegant Evening Bag (CONTINUED)

Construction (CONTINUED)

4-Thread Overlock	
Needles: Left, Right	
Wave/Overlock: Overlock	
Stitch Width: M	
Stitch Length: 2.0 - 3.0	
Stitch Selector: A	
Differential: N (normal)	
Foot: Utility	

- Serge one long side of the organza strip with a 3-thread rolled edge stitch.

- Thread the serger for a 4-thread overlock stitch using four cones of serger thread.

- Cut the tucked fabric into two 7" squares making sure to keep tucks evenly spaced on each piece.

- Attach a piping foot.

- Cover the Micro Welt Cord® with the satin bias strip and stitch. (See page 36.)

url on page 28

- Attach the covered cord to the bag front starting 1" below the top edge.
Note: Scan the QR code to the right for a video tutorial on attaching the piping.

- Angle the cording as you start to ease the cord onto the bag.

- Stitch for about 2".

- Stop and clip to the cord ¼" from the bottom of the bag.

- Holding the cording out of the way, continue stitching to the bottom of the bag front.

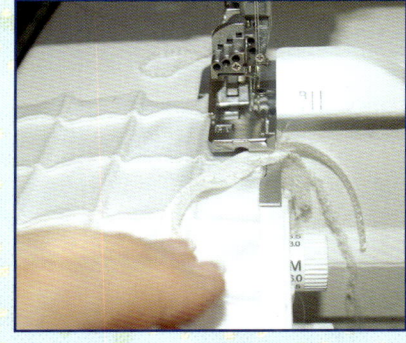

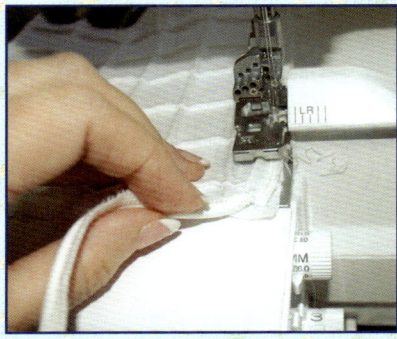

- Stitch all the way off of the bag corner leaving a few inches of thread attached so you have something to help start stitching on the bottom edge. (See page 36 for piping.)

- In order to continue attaching the cording to the bag front, turn the bag front and cording 90°.

- Use a stiletto to push back on the cording.

- Stitch until you are close to the next corner.

- Clip and turn as you did for the previous corner.

- Stitch the other side until cording is 1" from the top and then angle the cording off of the bag.

Construction (CONTINUED)

- Pin the twisted cord to each side of the bag just above the beginning and the end of the cording.

- Tie the twisted cord into one or more knots at ends to help keep it from catching in the stitching and slipping out.

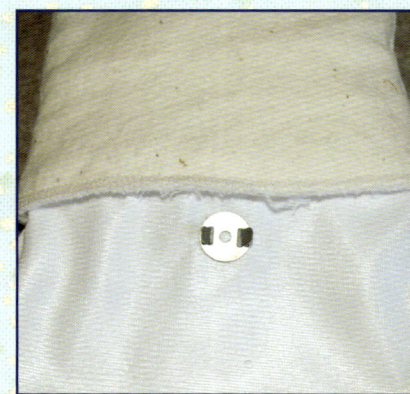

- Place the bag front and bag back pieces RST and stitch the bag together along each side and the bottom. If you stitch with the front side up, you can easily follow the stitching that attached the cording to the bag front.

- Turn the bag right side out. Fold the piece of batting in half forming a square and stitch the two sides.

4-Thread Overlock
Needles: Left, Right
Wave/Overlock: Overlock
Stitch Width: M
Stitch Length: 2.0 - 3.0
Stitch Selector: A
Differential: N (normal)
Foot: Utility

- Adjust the 4-thread overlock stitch for gathering by chaging the stitch length to 4 and the differential to 2.

- Gather the unfinished edge of the organza strip.

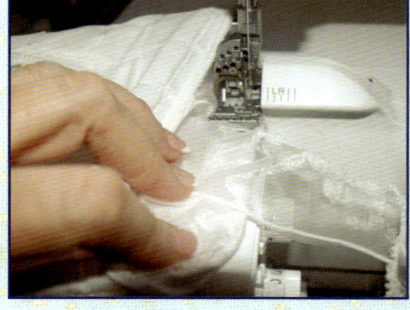

- Reset for balanced stitch with stitch length of 2-3 and differential on N.

- Insert the batting into the bag and stitch together around the top edge, aligning the batting and the outside edge.

- Turn the bag inside out. Attach the ruffle to the top edge of the bag. Angle the ruffle strip as you start and stop.

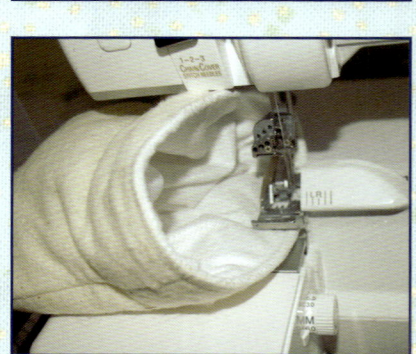

Note: Scan the QR code to the left for a video tutorial on attaching the ruffle.

url on page 28

- Continue to attach the ruffle until you have two to three layers of ruffle.

NOTE: The number of layers will depend on how tightly you were able to gather the fabric.

Elegant Evening Bag (CONTINUED)

Construction (CONTINUED)

- Fuse the Fantasic Fusible Fabric Backing® to the wrong side of the lining and fold the lining fabric in half forming a square.

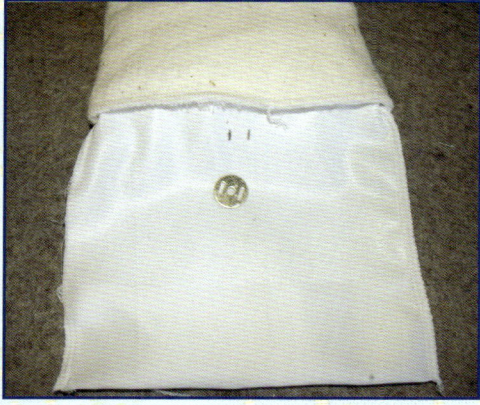

- Stitch the other side leaving a 2" opening in the center of the side.

- Insert the lining into the bag RST with the outside of the bag. Align the side seams.

- Stitch around the top edge making sure that the gathers do not get caught in the stitching. Pull the lining out of the bag.

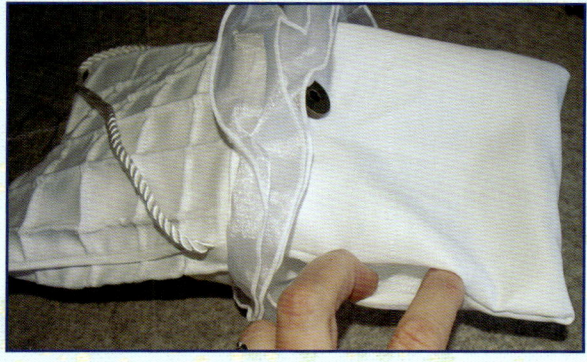

- Mark for placement of the magnetic closure using a FriXion® pen and the backing plate or metal support piece included with the closure.

- Attach the magnetic closure to the lining and repeat with the other half of the closure on the other side of the bag by going in through the lining.

- Using the opening in the lining, turn the bag right side out.

- Close the opening in the lining with double stick tape and push the lining into the bag.

Serge Protector by Betty

Just what you need, a beautiful cover for your wonderful machine! It features large pockets on three sides and a top zipper closure which will allow you to carry your serger covered. The Serge Protector comes in two sizes: one for large sergers such as the Triumph and Ovation, and a smaller one that can fit the Evolution, Enlighten and Imagine. The basic design is enhanced with several different techniques described in the pattern. As always, you can make it your own with your choice of decorative techniques!

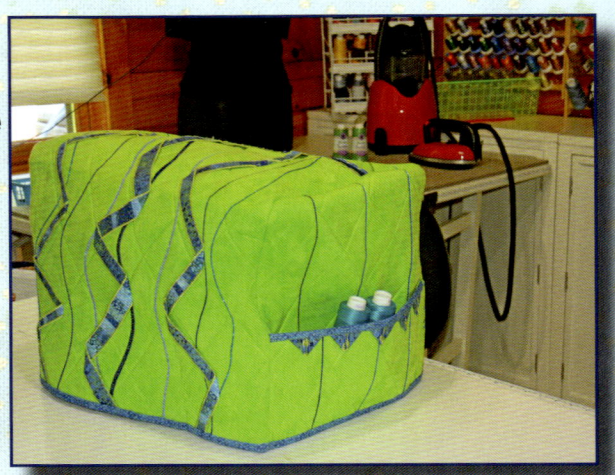

Supplies

- Outside fabric for large cover - 1 yard of 60" wide or 1¾ yard of 44" wide
- Outside fabric for small cover - ⅞ yard of either 60" or 44" wide fabric
- Lining fabric - same as outside fabric for the specific size cover
- Super Shaping Foam® Double Side Fusible – one large package for either cover (36" x 58")
- ⅓ yard each of two different fabrics that coordinate with the outside fabric
- ¼ yard of Lite Steam-a-Seam®
- Decorative serger threads – the sample cover used a combination of threads from Lamé Stylo, WonderFil™ (Razzle™ and Dazzle™), Madeira Decora 12
- Basting tape
- Serger cone thread to match outside fabric
- Zipper tape and two slides – 22" for large cover or 16" for small cover
- 7 Corner Ruler® by the Sew Sisters

Construction

- Fuse outside fabric and lining fabric to the Super Shaping Foam®

- For the 60" wide fabric, quilting is easier if you have smaller sections to work with. Cut the fused fabric and foam into three sections.
  Cut lengthwise - two sections at 22" wide and the third at 15" wide.
  NOTE: Quilting the fabric for the smaller cover can be done on a sewing machine as there is less room to maneuver on the Evolution and a chain stitch is not available on the Enlighten or the Imagine.

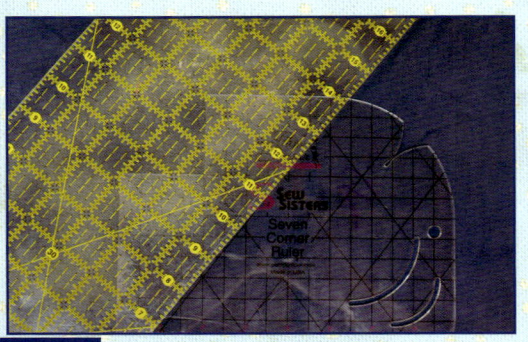

- Mark horizontal and vertical quilting lines on the front and back pieces. (The quilting lines on the 7 Corner Ruler® were used for the sample.)

  Note: All seams are ¼" unless otherwise noted.

Clutches and Covers

Serge Protector (CONTINUED)

Construction (CONTINUED)

- Thread your serger for a chain stitch - center needle using matching or coordinating thread.

- Attach the quilting bar and cover chain stitch foot to the Triumph or Ovation at the widest point possible.

- Stitch on the two marked quilting lines.

Chain Stitch - Center
Needles: Center
Wave/Overlock: N/A
Stitch Width: N/A
Stitch Length: 2.5
Stitch Selector: N/A
Differential: N (normal)
Foot: Cover/Chain
Attach Sewing Table

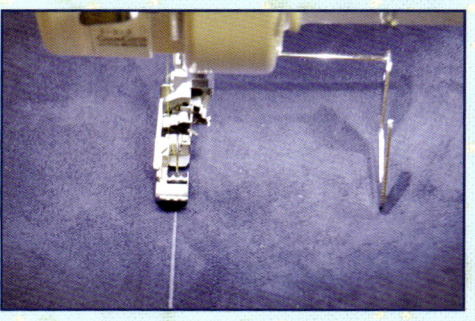 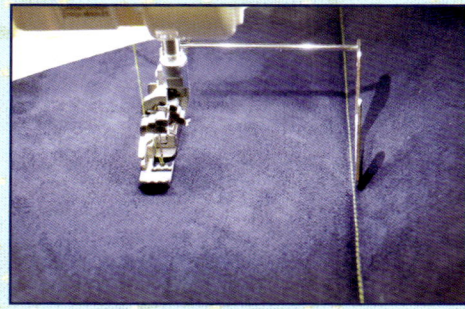 

- Continue quilting by aligning the quilting bar with the previous row of stitching.
  NOTE: The quilting bar works just as well when placed on the left side of the needle when there is too much fabric on the right side.)

- Once the fabric is quilted, use the appropriate pattern layout shown below. Cut and label the pieces of the cover.

Triumph and Ovation: 60" wide fabric

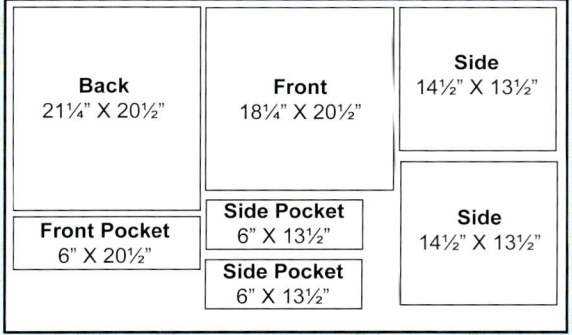

Evolution, Enlighten, Imagine: 45" wide Fabric

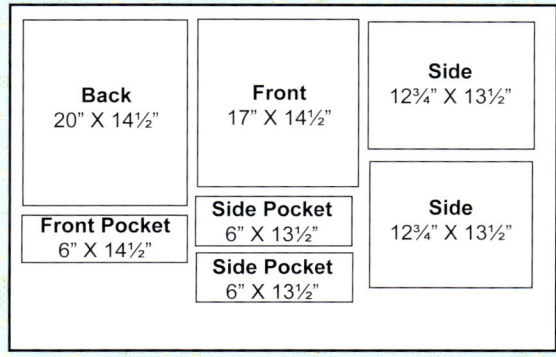

Triumph and Ovation: 45" wide fabric

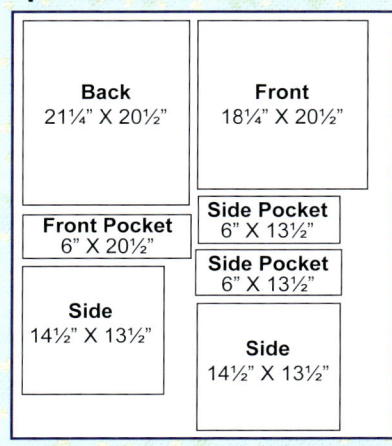

- Using the 7 Corner Ruler®, mark a 3" curve on the upper right corner of one side piece and the upper left corner of the other side piece.

- Mark a 1½" curve on the other upper corner of each piece.

- When you are ready to assemble the cover, the 3" curves are placed at the front of the side pieces.

Serge Protector (CONTINUED)

Construction (CONTINUED)
- Cut several pieces of decorative thread 2½ times the height of the back.

- Fold the threads in half and then twist them to create a rope.

- Tie a knot in each end.

- Repeat two more times, or see page 21 for twisted rope.
  - Thread the serger for chain stitch center with serger cone thread.

  - Attach a curve foot.

  - Couch the thread ropes to the bag front, curving back and forth from top to bottom.

  - Do not cut off the knots. They will be cut off as the top and bottom edges are finished.

Chain Stitch - Center	
Needles: Center	
Wave/Overlock: N/A	
Stitch Width: N/A	
Stitch Length: 2.0 - 3.0	
Stitch Selector: N/A	
Differential: N (normal)	
Foot: Curve	
Attach Sewing Table	

- Rethread the chain stitch looper with heavy decorative thread.

- Stitch with the lining fabric facing up.

- Wavy lines were stitched on the back, front pocket and the front.
  Front pocket - one color looper thread was used.
  Back - two different color threads were used.
  Front - three different color threads were used.

Cover Stitch - Narrow Right	
Needles: Center, Right	
Wave/Overlock: N/A	
Stitch Width: N/A	
Stitch Length: 2.0 - 3.0	
Stitch Selector: N/A	
Differential: N (normal)	
Foot: Curve	
Attach Sewing Table	

- Straight lines were stitched on the side and side pockets with two different color looper threads.
  NOTE: If you butt the top edge of the side pockets to the bottom edge of the sides and stitch, your lines will match when the pocket is in place on the cover.

- Thread the serger for cover stitch narrow right with serger cone thread in the needles and heavy decorative thread in the loopers.

- Stitch wavy lines with the lining facing up.
  Use two different colors on the front pocket. Use two different colors on the back.

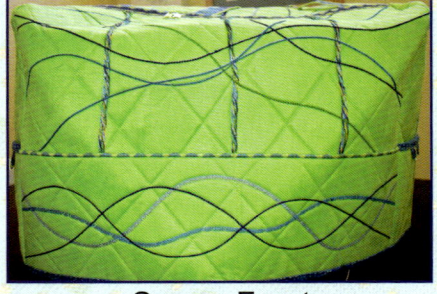
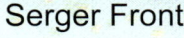

Serger Front

Serger Sides

Serger Back

Serge Protector (CONTINUED)

Construction (CONTINUED)

- Cut a strip of fabric 3" x WOF from each of the coordinating fabrics.

- Fuse the strips WST using the Lite Steam-a-Seam®.

- Thread the serger for a rolled edge stitch with a decorative thread in the upper looper.

- Stitch a rolled edge stitch on one long edge of the fused fabric.

- Move the rolled edge stitch to the left of the foot and using the foot as a guide stitch again creating one piece of fabric ribbon.

- Stitch a rolled edge stitch on one long edge of the remaining strip of fabric.

- Move the fabric strip to the left far enough to create a piece of fabric ribbon that is 1¼" wide.

- Repeat this to create another piece that is ¾" wide.

3-Thread Rolled Edge
Needles: Right
Wave/Overlock: Overlock
Stitch Width: 5.0
Stitch Length: 1R
Stitch Selector: D
Differential: N (normal)
Foot: Utility
Attach Sewing Table

url on page 28

- Arrange the fabric ribbons on the back.

- Pin the ribbons in place every time they are folded.

- Use basting tape on the top edge to hold ribbons in place until the top edge is finished.

Note: Scan the QR code on the right for a video tutorial on the folded ribbons.

- Thread the serger for the wave stitch with serger cone thread in the needle and decorative thread in the loopers. Lamé Stylo® thread was used in the cover pictured here.

- Using one of the coordinating fabrics, cut a 2½" strip x WOF.

- Using the directions on page 9 for the prairie point block, create ten prairie points.

- Arrange five prairie points on each side pocket.

- Clip them in place and set aside.

- Wave stitch across the top edge of the front pocket.

Wave Stitch
Needles: Right
Wave/Overlock: Wave
Stitch Width: 5.0
Stitch Length: Varies*
Stitch Selector: B
Differential: N (normal)
Foot: Utility
*depends on thread used

Clutches and Covers

Construction (CONTINUED)

- Adjust the wave stitch as follows: needle left, stitch selector A, stitch width 7.5. These settings will create a wider stitch.

- Separate the zipper tape into two pieces.

- Place one side of the tape with the teeth facing up on the top edge of the back piece and the other piece of zipper tape teeth up on the top of the front of the cover.

- Attach a cording foot.

- Wave stitch the zipper to the top edges of the front and back.
  NOTE: If you think you need more thread coverage just stitch over the first stitching.

- Thread the serger for a chain stitch left.

- Attach a cover chain foot.

- Stitch the fabric ribbon to the back of the cover at each of the folds.

Chain Stitch - Left
Needles: Left
Wave/Overlock: N/A
Stitch Width: N/A
Stitch Length: 2.0 - 3.0
Stitch Selector: N/A
Differential: N (normal)
Foot: Cover/Chain
Attach Sewing Table

- Turn the wave stitching on the edges of the zipper to the outside of the front.

- Stitch the left edge of the wave stitching to the front of the bag.
  NOTE: You should see the zipper teeth on the right side.

- For the pocket and bottom binding cut three strips 2¼" x WOF from one of the coordinating fabrics.

- For the side pocket binding fold one strip in half WST and press. Join the other two strips on one short end, press in half lengthwise and set aside.

- Align the binding strip on the top edge of the lining side of the side pocket.

- Stitch in place with a ⅜" seam allowance.

- Press the binding toward the top edge.

Clutches and Covers

Construction (CONTINUED)

- Press over to the front.

- Use basting tape to hold the binding in place for stitching.

- Chain stitch the binding in place, close to the left, folded edge.

- Thread the serger for a 4-thread overlock stitch.

- Attach the utility foot.

- Place the pockets on the sides and on the front of the cover.

- Stitch the sides and the bottom of each pocket to hold them in place.

4-Thread Overlock	
Needles:	Right, Left
Wave/Overlock:	Overlock
Stitch Width:	M
Stitch Length:	2.0 - 3.0
Stitch Selector:	A
Differential:	N (normal)
Foot:	Utility

- Connect the zipper pieces and then attach a zipper slide at each end of the zipper. (See page 42.)

- Lay the front/back section and the sides on the table in a cross shape. Make sure you have the sides in the correct position. The 3" curve on the top of each side piece should be facing the front of the cover.

- Attach a curve foot.

- Pick up one of the sides and the center section.

- Place them RST so that you can stitch with the side piece down on the serger.

- Stitch the center to the side, curving, adjusting as you stitch.
  NOTE: Holding the pieces together with clips may give you better control.

- Attach the other side in the same manner.

- Bind the bottom edge in the same manner as the side pockets. Connect the ends of the binding with your favorite method.

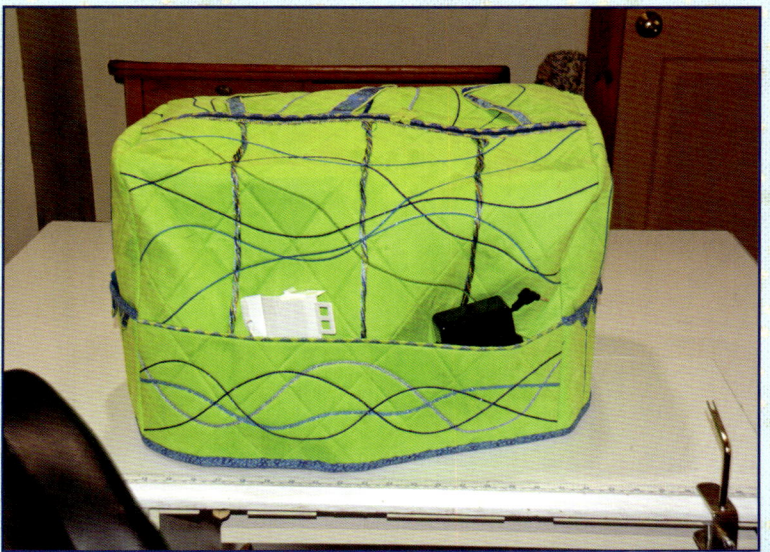

Techniques Tote by Pam

When we were ready to go to print with this book, we needed to add three more pages, so this is our "bonus project". This sweet little bag is big enough to hold your tablet, wallet, make-up and a few essentials. I literally made it from leftover pieces of fabric techniques and trims!

Supplies

- Two pieces of fabric cut 6½" x 27" for bag outside
- Two pieces of piping 27" long. (See page 36.)
- Optional: 27" of belt loop trim (See page 32.)
- 48" of 1" wide Flex & Firm® for the straps
- One piece of fabric 4" x 84" cut on the bias for pleated insert. (See pages 34 and 37.)
- Two pieces of fabric 3" x 28" for straps
- Four pieces of fabric 3" x 4" for strap tabs
- Four square rings for 1" straps
- 10" zipper tape and one slide
- Single Side Super Shaping Foam® 12½" x 27"
- Wonder Clips®
- Two pieces of plastic canvas cut 4" x 9"
- 5-in-1 Ruler® by Pam Damour

3-Thread Overlock - Wide	
Needle:	Left
Stitch Width:	7.5
Stitch Length:	2.5 - 3.0
Stitch Selector:	A
Differential:	1.0 or N (normal)
Foot:	Utility

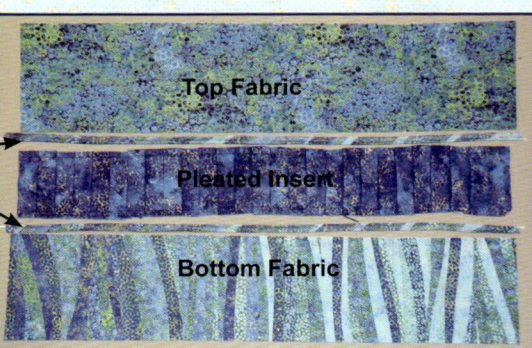

Piping — Top Fabric / Pleated Insert / Bottom Fabric

Construction (CONTINUED)

Bag Body

- Begin by preparing your outside pieces. Assemble as shown using the serger setting provided.

2" Strip of Top Fabric
Belt Loop Trim
Top Fabric
Pleated Insert
Bottom Fabric

- Optional: After all of these have been pieced together in this order, cut two-inch strip off the top fabric to insert the belt loop trim. Press flat.

  Note: I find it easier to sew the trim onto the bag body first and then add the extra two-inch strip.

- With wrong sides together, fuse the Super Shaping Foam®. With the 5-in-1 Ruler®, line up one long edge of the foam with the serging.

Construction (CONTINUED)

- Fold the bag in half with RST, lining up sides and bottom and serge.

- Align the center of the bottom seam with the center of the bag sides, with RST, forming a point.

- Sew across the end with a 4" seam with 2" on each side of the zipper. For accuracy, use the 45° angle lines on the 5-in-1 Ruler®. Turn right side out. Set aside.

3-Thread Overlock - Wide	
Needle: Left	
Stitch Width: 7.5	
Stitch Length: 2.5 - 3.0	
Stitch Selector: A	
Differential: 1.0 or N (normal)	
Foot: Utility, Cording/Piping	

Bag Lining

- Separate the zipper into two pieces and place on the bottom edge of the bag 2" in from each end.

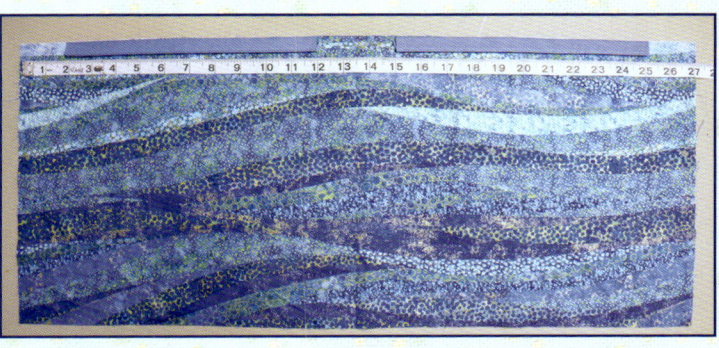

- Serge the zipper in place using the cording/piping foot. (See page 42.)

- Marry the zipper together by inserting the slide as shown on page 42. Leave the slide in the center of the zipper with both ends of the zipper closed.

- Align the center of the zipper with the center of the bag sides, with RST, forming a point.

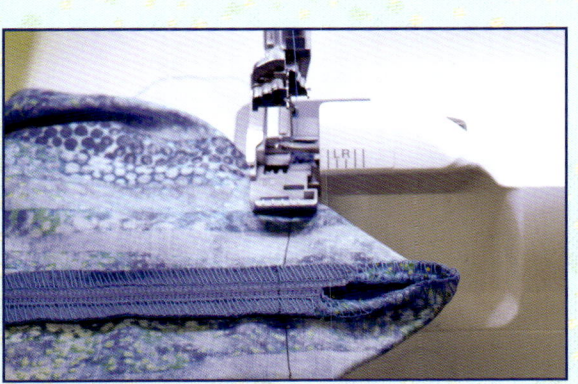

- Sew across the end as you did earlier with the bag. Set aside.

Techniques Tote (CONTINUED)

Construction (CONTINUED)
Straps

Chain Stitch - Center
Needles: Center
Stitch Length: 4.0
Stitch Width: N/A
Stitch Selector: N/A
Differential: N (normal)
Foot: Utility

- Fold one edge of your strap fabric over ½" and press. Fuse Flex & Firm® to the wrong side of the strap fabric with ½" of fabric extending. Press the bottom edge up and then the folded edge over, with ½" of fabric extending past the Flex & Firm®. Convert to chain stitch

- Repeat with the strap tabs.

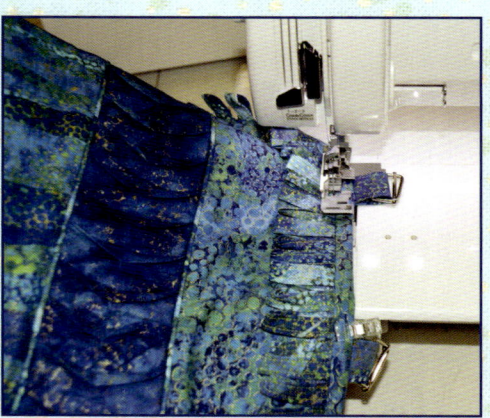

- Fold each strap tab in half crosswise, with the square ring in the fold. Wonder Clip® the bag strap tabs to the top edge of the bag.

- Turn the bag inside out. Lining up the one side seam and the centers of the four sides, pin the lining top edge to the bag top edge, RST. Convert back to a 3-thread overlock - wide. Serge all the way around the top edge. There is no need to leave an opening, because we have a zipper in the lining.

- Open the zipper in the lining and turn the bag right side out.

- Roll the outside fabric to inside toward the lining, with the seam about ½" from the top edge. The top edge of the back is now even with the top edge of the Super Shaping Foam inside the bag. Wonder Clip® in place.

- Convert back to a chain stitch, and stitch in the ditch along the top edge.

- Add the straps to the strap tabs, folding edges under ½" and 1" to the back. Chain stitch or top stitch using your sewing machine.

- Enjoy your new bag and feel free to add pockets, or other embellishments. For bag ideas, check out our book "Hold Everything".

All Squared Away

Pam's Serger Quilt by Pam

Yes, you can quilt with a serger! This quilt uses the 15 serger blocks, set on point. The black contrasting triangles complete the squares so that it can be seamed in the traditional manner. Blocks are sashed with two-inch sashing, and are surrounded by a three-inch border, mitered French binding and wave stitch piping. The finished size is approximately 38 ½" x 58 ½".

Supplies

- 15 - 6" technique blocks
- 2¼ yards of black background
- ½ yard of border fabric
- 1¾ yards of fabric for the backing
- ¾ yard of fabric for binding and wave stitch piping
- Two spools of 12 weight WonderFil™ thread for wave stitch piping to match the binding (Spagetti™ is what we used.)
- Lamé Stylo thread for quilting 🔵
- 40" x 60" quilt batting
- Micro-Stitch™ Basting Gun 🔵
- Wonder Clips®
- Permanent Double Stick Tape® 🔵

The blocks in this quilt are listed from left to right, top to bottom.

Make all blocks to finish as 6 ½" squares.

Top Row:
Ribbon and Lace Block (See page 20.)
Ric Rac and Rope (See page 21.)
Pintuck Block (See page 18.)

Second Row:
Serger Lace (See page 24.)
Box Pleated Windows (See page 12.)
Prairie Points (See page 19.)

Third Row:
Decorative Trims (See page 16.)
Ruffles and Waves (See page 22.)
Circles and Squares (See page 14.)

Fourth Row:
Cover Stitch Plaid (See page 15.)
Twisted Tucks (See page 26.)
Flatlock Lace (See page 17.)

Fifth Row:
Chain Stitch Ruffle (See page 13.)
Basket Weave (See page 10.)
Stitch and Scrunch (See page 25.)

Construction

- Cut 30 - 5½" squares (black) in half diagonally. The long bias edges will be sewn to each of the four sides of each technique block.

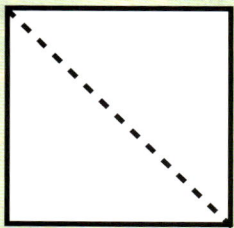

By constructing it this way, the blocks will have more stability because the outer sides will now have straight of grain edges.

3-Thread Overlock - Wide

Needle: Left
Stitch Width: 6.0
Stitch Length: 2.0
Stitch Selector: A
Differential: 1.0 or N (normal)
Foot: Utility or Open Toe

All Squared Away

Construction (CONTINUED)

- Stitch opposite sides first, with your serger stitch width set at 6.0, centering the triangles on the straight sides.

- Sew with the back side of the block up, RST.

- Press the seams flat toward the triangles. Serge the other two triangles, centering them on the remaining two straight sides.

- Press all seams, and trim if necessary, to a 9" block. When trimming, be sure to leave ¼" of black space at the center of each side.

Assembly

- Once you have completed all 15 blocks, it is time to start putting your top together.

- Arrange the blocks in your desired order.

- Cut 2½" wide sashing. You will need ten – 2½" x 9" pieces to make five rows of three blocks. Stitch the sashing on one side of two blocks in each row. Assemble each row by joining the three blocks together.

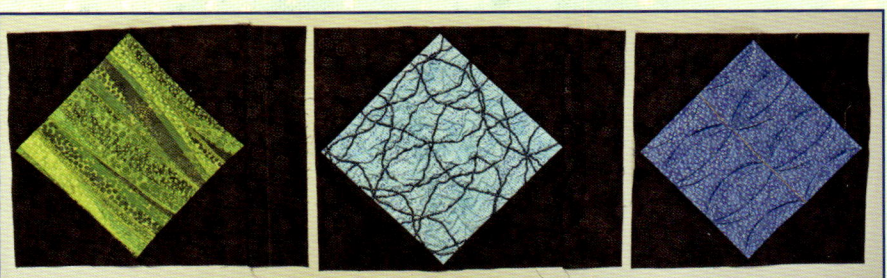

Assembly (CONTINUED)

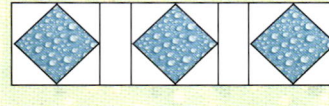

- Repeat this for the next four rows.

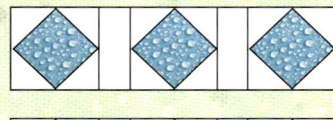

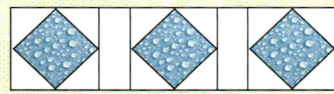

- Stitch the 2½" sashing between each row, joining the rows together. The sashing should be the width of the quilt.

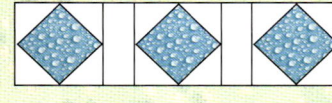

- Add a 2½" border of sashing around the entire quilt.

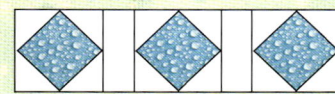

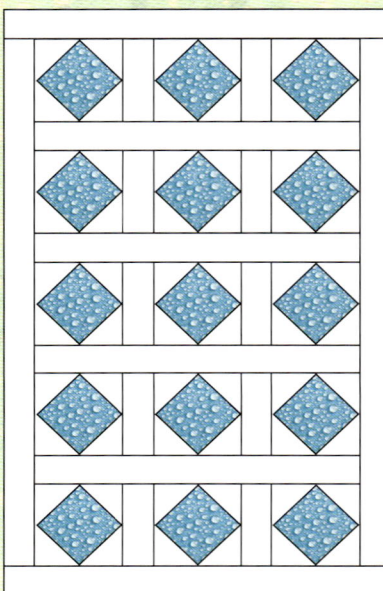

- Now add a 3" border around the entire sashed quilt.

- Make your quilt "sandwich" by layering the quilt top and the backing, with the batting in the middle. Make sure the batting and backing extend beyond the quilt by at least 3" all the way around to account for any shifting of the fabric.

Quilting

- Accordion fold (back and forth) the quilt on each side toward the center. If your serger has a chain stitch, quilt on your serger, or use your favorite quilting or tying method. I quilted mine by stitching in the ditch with Lamé Stylo thread in my needle and in the lower looper.

- After the quilting is completed, trim the backing and batting to match the quilt top.

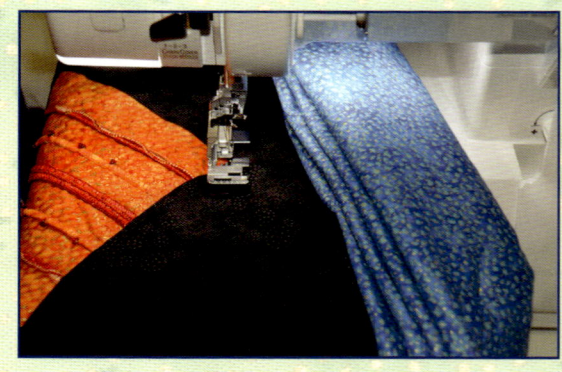

Pam's Serger Quilt (CONTINUED)

Binding

- Cut 200" of 3" bias for the binding. (See page 34.)
- Cut 200" of 1 ½" bias for the wave stitch.

Note: I chose to sew on my binding and wave stitch piping with my regular sewing machine. I used a piping foot because my serger does not have a foot with a piping groove that I can use when serging with a chain stitch.

Piping or Rolled Edge Piping

- If your serger has the wave stitch, make 200" of wave stitch piping (see page 41.). If not, make rolled edge piping (see page 39). Trim the seam allowance to ½", if necessary.

- Begin along the center of one of the long sides, leaving about 3" of loose trim and binding for the join.

- Pin or Wonder Clip® the serged piping to the edge of the quilt. With the binding folded in half with wrong sides together and raw edges along the side of the quilt, lay the binding on top of the serged piping. Stitch carefully, feeling for the edge of the wave piping under the binding, so that your stitch line is in the serged stitch line of the piping.

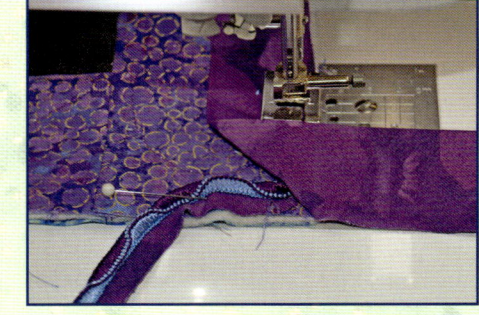

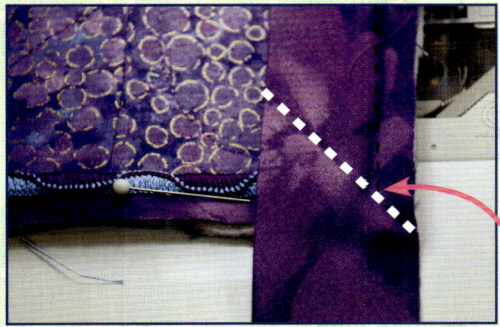

- Snip the piping seam allowance at the corners to allow it to turn. Pin it in place.

- Before you reach the corner, fold the binding at a 45° angle, as shown here. Make a crease with your fingernail

- Sew just up to the crease and back stitch.

- Fold back on the crease, then fold the binding back onto itself with the fold even with edge of the quilt.

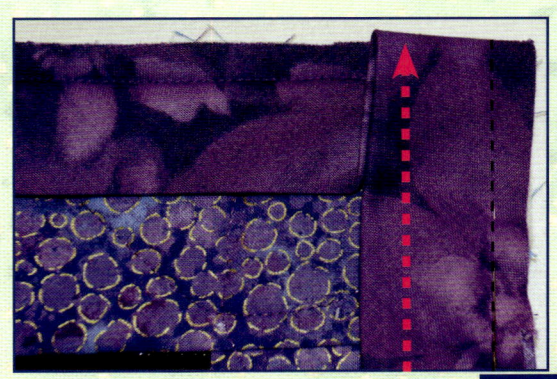

- Begin sewing at the folded edge and continue to sew, repeating this at the other three mitered corners.

Pam's Serger Quilt (CONTINUED)

Binding

Joining the Piping and Binding

- To join the piping, overlap the two ends as shown.
- To join the binding, fold the edge of the starting end to the inside so the raw edges do not show. Tuck the other edge of the binding inside the first edge and stitch in place.

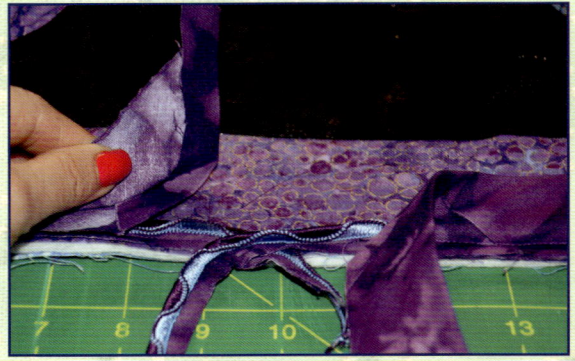

- Secure by hand stitching or using Permanent Double Stick Tape®.

- Wrap the folded edge of the binding around to the back side of the quilt and hand stitch in place or machine stitch in the ditch from the front.

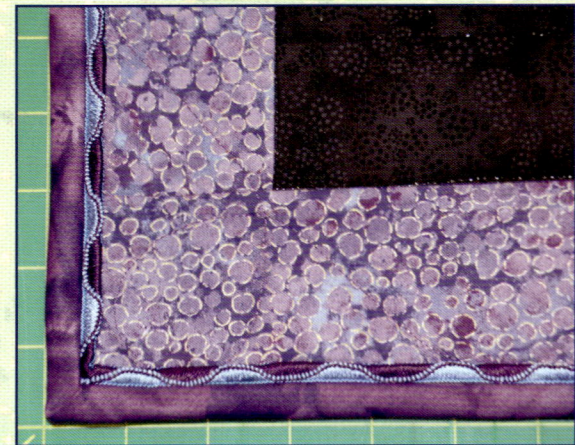

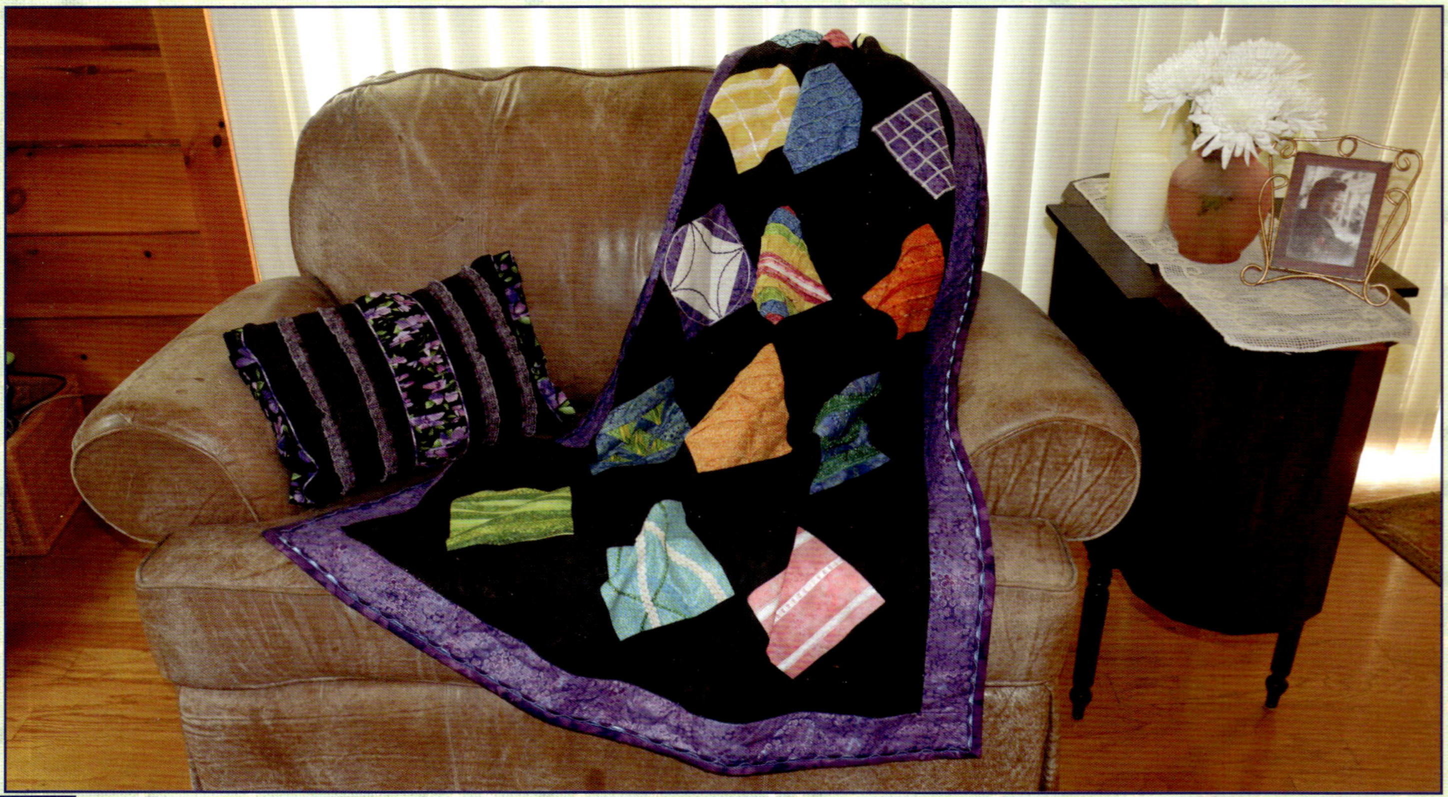

All Squared Away

Table Runner by Pam

Now that you have mastered a few of our serger techniques, it is time to use them to make something fun! This table runner can have as many or as few technique squares as you desire. Five blocks will make a runner 54" long; Four blocks will make a runner 45" long. Finished width is 11". All seams are ¼".

3-Thread Overlock - Wide
Needle: Right
Stitch Width: 6.0
Stitch Length: 2.5
Stitch Selector: A
Differential: 1.0 or N (normal)
Foot: Open Toe or BL

Supplies

- 5 - 6½" square technique blocks.
- ⅞ yard of quilting cotton
- 3¼ yards of Micro Welt Cord® 🪡 and one fat quarter to make piping or 3¼ yards of ready-made piping
- 12" x 56" quilt batting
- Optional: Permanent Double Stick Tape® 🪡
- Wonder Clips®

Layout

- Using the diagram to the right cut:
    three 13" squares
    one 9½" square
    two 12" x 28" runner back pieces

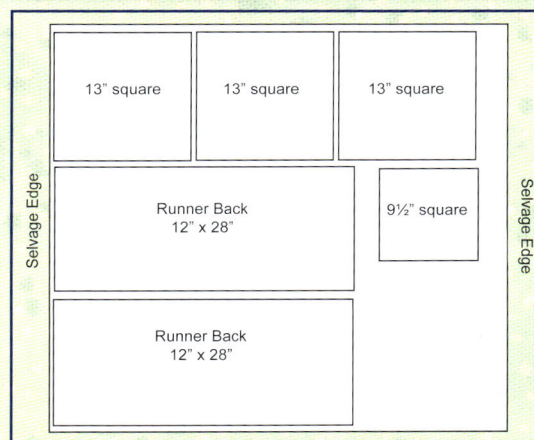

Construction

- Cut the three larger squares diagonally as shown to yield 12 large triangles; cut the small square diagonally to yield four smaller triangles.

Inner Blocks

- Assemble the inner blocks (those not at the ends) as shown. Using two of the large triangles, line up the straight grained edges to opposite sides of the technique block square, with the points of the triangles extending past the technique block. The points will be at opposite sides of the technique square.

- Press all seam allowances toward the triangle fabrics.

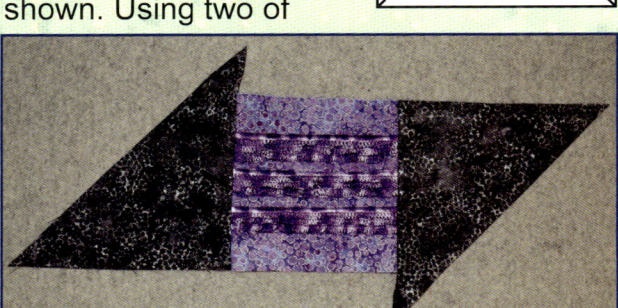

Table Runner (CONTINUED)

Inner Blocks (CONTINUED)

- Trim off the points even with the rest of the strip.

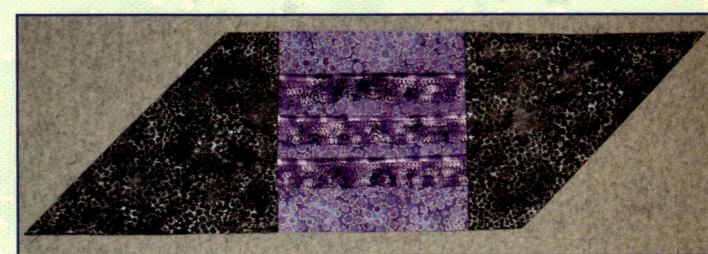

End Blocks

- On each end block, sew one larger triangle and one smaller triangle. Sew the longest side of the smaller triangle to the other side of the block.

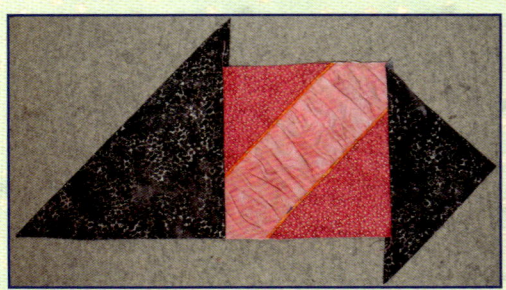

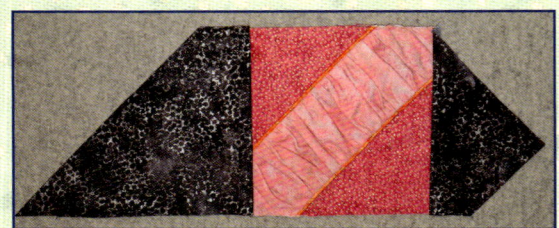

- Trim off the points even with the rest of the strip.

Runner Assembly

- Assemble your block strips and serge the rows together. The remaining small triangles will be sewn onto the angled ends, creating a squared off end.

- Add the two remaining large triangles at the ends to finish the runner top.

- Press all seams flat.

- If your runner sides are a bit uneven, don't panic! Trim evenly on both long edges. It is nearly impossible to determine the exact size of the runner as the size of your seam allowances may vary slightly. We have allowed ample fabric so it can be trimmed after the top is completed.

Runner Back

- With right sides together, serge both back pieces together end to end, so that you have a center seam, and it is long enough to line the front.

- With right sides together, layer the runner back with the runner top, and the trim back to match the top.

- Cut your batting to match both layers.

Table Runner (CONTINUED)

Construction (CONTINUED)

Piping Trim

3-Thread Overlock - Wide
Needle: Right
Stitch Width: 6.0
Stitch Length: 2.5
Stitch Selector: A
Differential: 1.0 or N (normal)
Foot: Open Toe or BL

- If you are making your own piping, please turn to page 36 for complete instructions.

- Start the piping along one long side of the runner front.

- Stop sewing about 2" before each corner without removing the project from serger.

- Clip the seam allowance of the piping about ⅜" from the corner so piping will turn.

- As you approach the corner, bend the piping 90° as shown and serge right off the edge.

- Bring the project back to the serger at the corner and begin serging the next side.

- Serge all the way around and allow about a 2½" overlap. Remove excess Micro Welt Cord® before serging. (See page 36.)

- Join by overlapping the flat ends of the piping where you removed the cord.

- Create a "sandwich", layering the top and back with right sides together. Layer the batting to the back side. Wonder Clip® or pin all the layers together.

- Begin serging along one of the long sides allowing about a 7" opening to turn right sides out.

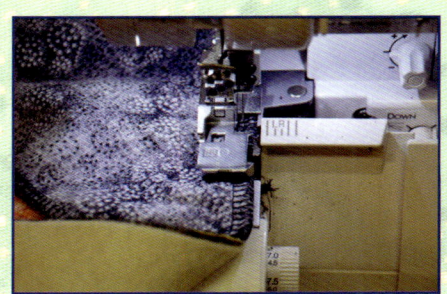

- Serge the corners by going off the ends, and then back on, just as you did when applying the piping.

- Turn right side out and press flat. Secure opening with Permanent Double Stick Tape®, or hand stitch closed.

Betty's Serger Quilt by Betty

The Serger Quilts represent the 'Heart' of this book. The 15 technique squares and several other serger techniques are combined into a beautiful showpiece that you can accomplish with your serger!

Supplies

- 15 technique squares
- 15 - 6½" squares of background fabric (⅝ yard)
- ⅓ yard of coordinating fabric for first border
- ¼ yard of first border fabric for wave piping
- ½ yard of coordinating fabric for second border
- ⅓ yard of fabric for binding
- 1½ yards of backing fabric
- One package of crib size quilt batting
- Two spools of decorative thread for wave piping (WonderFil™ Razzle™ and Dazzle™ were used for the sample.)
- Serger cone threads to coordinate with your fabrics
- FriXion® pen 🧷
- Micro Stitch™ basting gun 🧷
- Wonder Clips®

3-Thread Overlock - Wide	
Needle:	Right
Wave/Overlock:	Overlock
Stitch Width:	M
Stitch Length:	2.0 - 3.0
Stitch Selector:	A
Differential:	N (normal)
Foot:	Utility

Construction

- Using the techniques in this book, create 15 technique squares (shown in blue in the diagrams). If you wish to create a larger quilt you can always duplicate your squares and/or create larger squares.

- Set aside eight of the background squares, shown in white.

- Cut the next six background squares on the diagonal creating 12 triangles.

- Cut the remaining background square into quarter square triangles.

- Arrange the background fabrics and the technique squares as shown.

- Using a 3-thread overlock - wide stitch and ¼" seam allowance stitch together the squares and triangles into diagonal rows as shown.

- Join the diagonal rows to complete the center of the quilt top.

- For the first border, cut four strips 2" x WOF.

All Squared Away

Construction (CONTINUED)

- Use diagonal seams to join the strips into one long piece. Align the strips as shown. Draw a stitching line from the upper left to the lower right corner.

- Stitch on this line, cutting off the small triangle shown to the right in the picture.

- Press the seams to one side.

- Using the ¼ yd. of coordinating fabric and the instructions on page 34, create eight yards of 1" wide bias.

- Fold and press the bias fabric in half, WST.

- Thread the serger for the wave stitch with decorative thread in the loopers and cone thread in the right needle. If your machine does not have a wave stitch, thread for a 3-thread overlock - wide, using the same threads as indicated for the wave stitch.

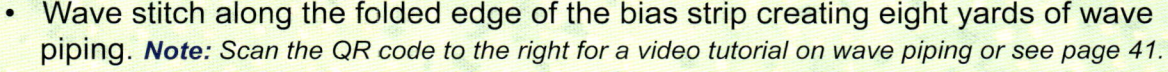

Wave Stitch
Needle: Right
Wave/Overlock: Wave
Stitch Width: 5.0 - 7.5
Stitch Length: 1.0 - 2.0
Stitch Selector: B
Differential: N (normal)
Foot: Utility
Check that threads are in the correct tension slots for wave.

- Wave stitch along the folded edge of the bias strip creating eight yards of wave piping. *Note: Scan the QR code to the right for a video tutorial on wave piping or see page 41.*

url on page 28

Chain Stitch - Right
Needle: Right
Stitch Length: 3.0
Differential: N (normal)
Foot: Cover/Chain
Use matching cone thread in needle and chainstitch looper

- Using a chain stitch - right and a cover chain stitch foot, attach the wave piping to both sides of the first border strip. You should be stitching right next to the right edge of the wave stitching.

- Once the wave piping is applied, cut the border strips for the two long sides of the quilt.

- Use Wonder Clips® to hold the borders on the quilt while you stitch.

- Attach the side borders with a chain stitch. Stitch with the border strip on top and stitch right on top of the stitching that attached the wave piping.

  NOTE: In order to ensure that the piping is not caught in the seam, go slowly and stitch right on top of the stitching that attached the piping to the border strip.

- Press seams toward the center of the quilt.

- Repeat for the top and bottom border strips.

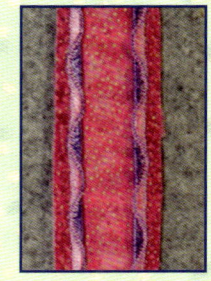

Betty's Serger Quilt (CONTINUED)

Construction (CONTINUED)

- For the second border, cut five strips 3" x WOF and join with diagonal seams creating one long border strip as you did for the first border.

- Cut the borders for the long sides.

- Clip the second border strips to the first border and stitch with the first border on top so that you can again stitch through the stitching that attached the piping to the border.

- Press seams toward the second border.

- Repeat for the second borders on the top and bottom.

- Sandwich the batting between the quilt top and backing.

- Use the Micro Stitch™ basting gun to hold the layers together.

- Using a FriXion® pen, mark quilting lines on both diagonals of each background square.

- For quilting, move the needle to the center position.
  Note: Scan the QR code to the right for a video tutorial on serger quilting.

- To secure the beginning of your quilting, start 1" from the border and stitch back to the border.

- Then, with the needle in the fabric, pivot the quilt so you can stitch on the marked line.

url on page 28

- When you reach the end of the line at the opposite border pivot again and stitch for 1" on top of your original stitches.

- Cut four strips of the binding fabric 2¼" x WOF and stitch them together with diagonal seams, as you did earlier.

- Press in half with WST. Move the needle to the left position.

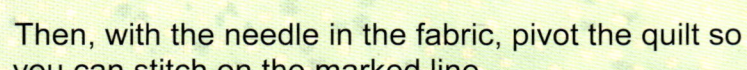

- Stitch the binding to the back of the quilt, aligning the quilt and binding with the edge of the cover chain foot. Miter at the corners. (See page 77.)

- Use your favorite method to connect the ends of the binding, or see page 78.

- Press the binding to the outside and then wrap it around to the front.

- Chain stitch the binding to the front of the quilt aligning the left edge of the foot with the folded edge of the binding.

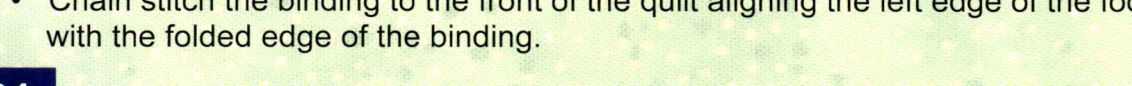

Sampler Pillow by Pam

This pillow is made with four technique squares. They are the Pleated Windows, Lace, Prairie Points and Pintucks. Finish size is 14" square.

Supplies

- ⅛ yard of contrasting fabric for sashing
- ½ yard of fabric for pillow back, pleated window block and welting.
- Three coordinating fat quarters
- Two yards of Valance Welt Cord® (for piping)
- 15" of zipper tape and one slide
- 14" pillow form or Pam's Perfect Puff & Stuff®
- Stiletto

Construction

Backing, Welting and Pleated Windows:
Cut your fabric as shown:
　　　Pillow back: 15" x 17"
　　　Pleated windows: 7" x 22"
　　　Bias for welting: approximately 66" x 2" wide.

Pintuck Technique Square: See page 18.

Serger Lace Technique Square: See page 24.

Prairie Point Technique Square: See page 19.

Box Pleated Windows Square: See page 12.

Bias for Welting / Bias for Welting / Pleated Windows / Bias for Welting	Pillow Back 15" x 17"

4-Thread Overlock - Wide
Needle: Right, Left
Stitch Width: 6.0
Stitch Length: 2.5
Stitch Selector: A
Differential: N (normal)
Foot: Utility

Pillow Front Construction

- After each technique square is completed, trim all squares to 6½"

- Cut the sashing 1½" wide. Cut six strips 1½" x 6½". Serge each of these strips to the top and bottom edges of each block, as shown to the left.

- Cut three strips of sashing 1½" x 15" and serge the pillow front together as shown to the right, one sashing between the two pieces and one on each outside edge.

Sampler Pillow (CONTINUED)

Construction (CONTINUED)

Pillow Back/Zipper Insertion

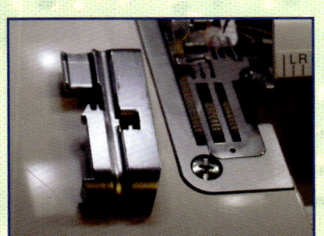

- Trim 2" off the long side of back so that you have a 15" square and a 2" x 15" strip (placket).

- Separate the zipper and using the cording/piping foot, serge one side to the zipper placket and one side to the zipper back, with right sides together and teeth side down. (See page 42.)

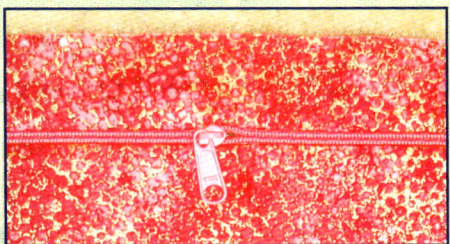

- Bring the slide to the middle of the pillow, and leave both ends of the zipper closed.

- Set aside.

Piping (See piping technique on page 36.)

Note: Piping can be easily made with your serger. You can also use your serger to attach ready-made piping.

4-Thread Overlock - Wide
Needle: Right, Left
Stitch Width: 6.0
Stitch Length: 2.5
Stitch Selector: A
Differential: N (normal)
Foot: Utility

- Serge your three pieces of bias together with diagonal seams as seen on page 31, and make piping using the directions on page 36.

- When serging the piping onto the pillow front, start and stop at the center of the bottom edge.

- To turn corners, snip the seam allowance of the piping ½" before the corner and bend the piping, holding it in place with a stiletto.

- Serge off the end and start back on the corner.

- To join the piping at the bottom edge, leave about 2" extra at each end and overlap as shown.

- If using premade piping, serge the piping to right side of the fabric.

- Pin the pillow front to the pillow back, with any excess length of the pillow back extending off the bottom.

- Serge all the way around, using the piping foot, and trimming any excess off the pillow back.

- Pull the zipper slide open, turn right sides out and stuff!

Just For Fun!

Pretty (Easy) Pillowcase by Pam

This pillow case can be made two ways, using the standard method and the "burrito" method. Choose which way you like best, or make both!

Supplies
- Main fabric: ¾ yd of 44/45" cotton fabric
- Hem fabric: ¼ yd of 44/45" cotton fabric
- Trim fabric: 2" strip of 44/45" cotton fabric
- Thread to match the main body of pillowcase

Cut
- Pillowcase body: cut one 27" long by the full width of 44/45" cotton fabric and trim off the selvages
- Pillowcase hem fabric: cut one 9" by 44"
- Trim fabric: cut one 2" by 44"

4-Thread Overlock
Needle: Right, Left
Stitch Width: 6.5 & 7.5
Stitch Length: 3.0
Stitch Selector: A
Differential: 1.0 or N (normal)
Foot: Utility or Open Toe

Construction

- Press the trim fabric (green) in half lengthwise with wrong sides together. Place it along the end of the pillowcase body fabric, serging both layers together across the WOF.

- Serge using a 4-thread overlock stitch with a 6.5 stitch width, with raw edges together, serging selvage to selvage.

- Press the hem fabric lengthwise in half, wrong sides together.

- Serge three fabrics together layering the trim between the hem and the main fabric with RST, and a 7.5 stitch width. Use your previous stitching line as a guide.

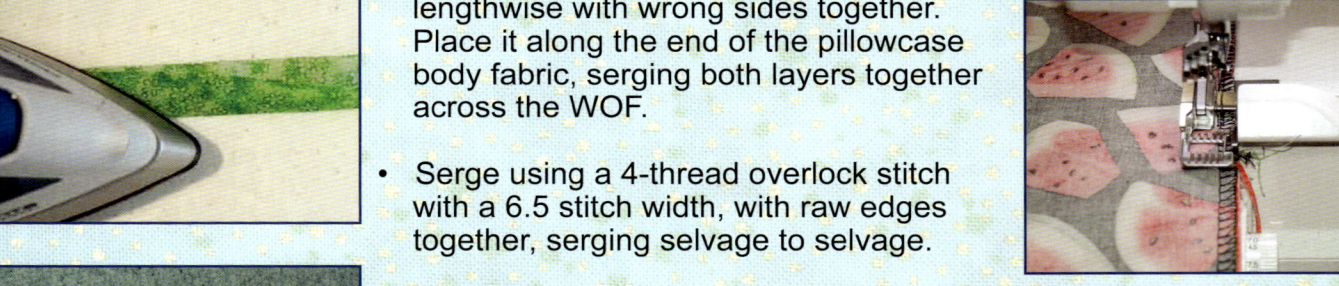

- Press the seam flat to one side.

- If one of the fabrics is narrower than the others, trim to the smallest section.

- Fold the pillowcase in half, lining up at the seams. Serge along the end and side with a 7.5 stitch width.

Construction (CONTINUED)

- To turn the corner, serge to end of the pillowcase and stop.

- Make one stitch off the end. Lift the presser foot and pull your fabric off the stitch fingers.

- Pivot and put the fabric back under the foot, lining up the serged end with the needles.

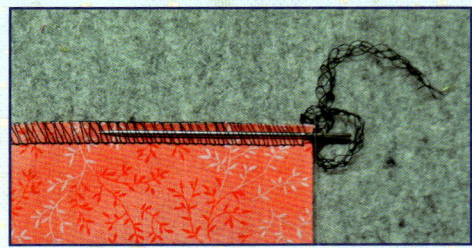

- To finish, leave a serger "tail" and use a large darning needle or bodkin to draw the excess thread inside the seam. Trim off the excess thread.

The Burrito Method to make a Pillow Case

- Begin as you would with the previous pillowcase by cutting all the pieces, pressing the accent strip in half, and serging it onto pillow body.

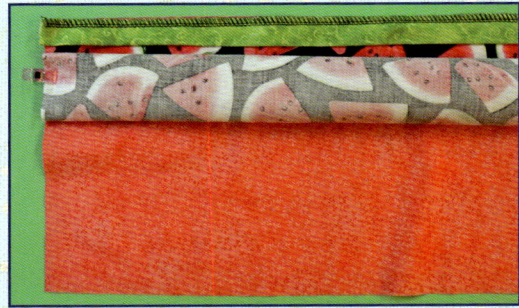

- Starting at unserged end of the pillowcase, roll the fabric toward the serged end. Stop right before you get to the flat piping.

- With your pillowcase "roll' in the center, and right sides together, pin or Wonder Clip® both hem edges with the serged edge in the center. Serge all layers together with a 7.5 stitch width seam.

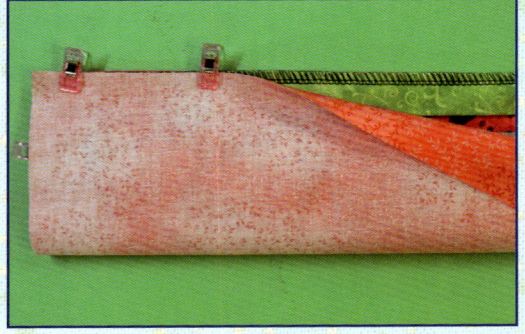

- Pull your roll out from the center turning right sides out.

- Press flat.

- Trim off the width to the narrowest fabric.

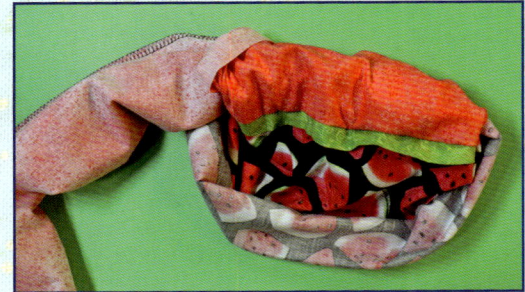

- Fold in half, sew the end and side the same as the previous project and pull the serger "tail" inside the seam.

Heirloom Pillowcase by Betty

When you combine the techniques found in the ribbon and lace block with the gathers and edging in the ruffles and waves block, you can easily create this delicate pillowcase. It will quickly become a family treasure for years to come!

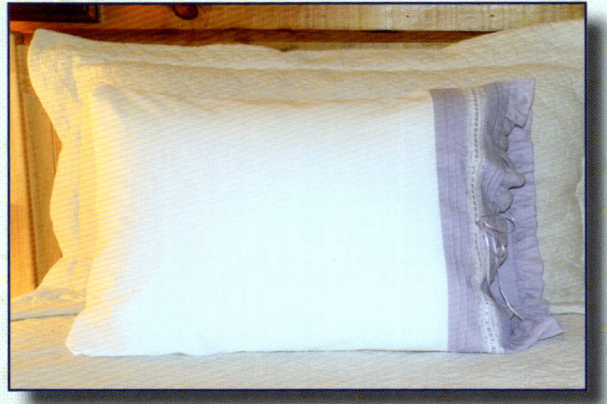

Supplies

- ¾ yard of white batiste for main body
- ⅝ yard of pastel colored batiste for band and ruffle
- Four spools of white serger cone thread
- Two spools of serger cone thread to match the band
- One spool of machine embroidery thread to match the band
- 1¼ yards of lace insertion
- 1¼ yards of ladder trim
- 1½ yards of silk or satin ribbon to thread through the ladder trim

3-Thread Rolled Edge

Needle: Right
Wave/Overlock: Overlock
Stitch Width: M
Stitch Length: 1 (rolled edge)
Stitch Selector: D
Differential: N (normal)
Foot: Utility, Ruffle

Construction

- Using the pastel colored batiste, cut the band and ruffle as follows:

  one strip: 6" x WOF; one strip: 8" x WOF; two strips: 2" x WOF.

- Press the 6" strip in half lengthwise WST.

- Press each long flat and cut edge to the middle crease, as if you were making flat bias tape.

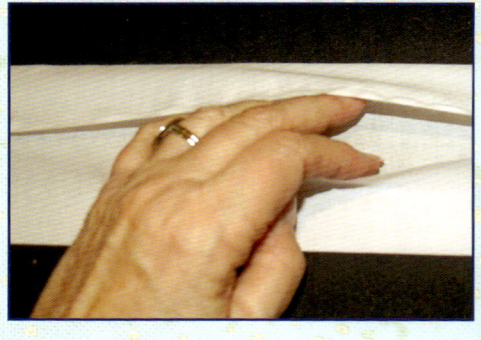

- Thread the serger for a 3-thread rolled edge stitch. Use matching cone thread in the lower looper and the needle, and machine embroidery thread in the upper looper.

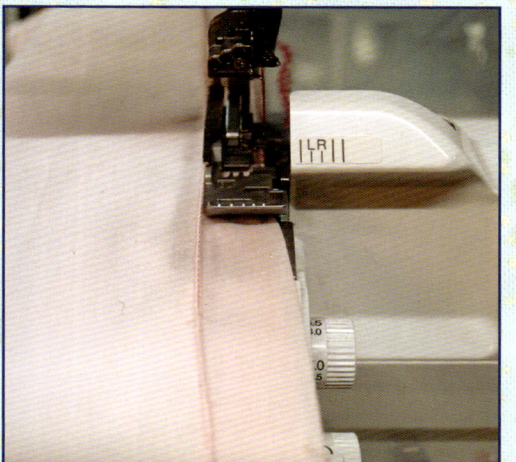

- Keeping the edges of the 6" strip turned under and the right side of the fabric facing up, stitch a 3-thread rolled edge along each of the outside folds.

- Fold again between the first row of rolled edge stitching and the cut edge in order to stitch a second row of rolled edge pintuck parallel to the first. Space this fold so that it is the width of your presser foot from the first row.

NOTE: The foot width varies depending on your machine. Scan the QR code to the right for a video tutorial on rolled edge pintucks

url on page 28

Just For Fun!

Construction (CONTINUED)

- Repeat for the other side of the fabric strip.

- Press tucks toward the cut edge.

- Using a rolled edge stitch with RST, join the short ends of the 2" x WOF strips to form a circle.

- Stitch a rolled edge on the right side of one side of the fabric circle. Set aside.

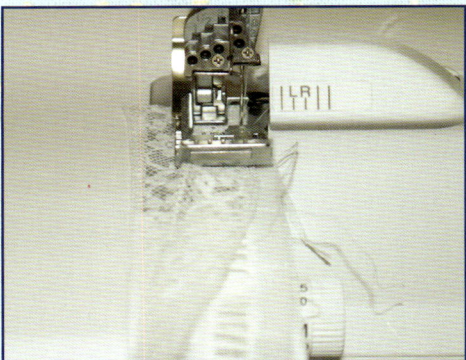

- Re-thread the serger for a rolled edge stitch with three spools of white cone thread.

- With wrong sides together, attach a piece of lace insertion on each side of the ladder trim. Be sure to just catch the lip of the lace and the edge of the ladder as close as possible to the 'ladder' stitches. Press.

- Cut the band fabric in two along the center crease.

- Using these new cut edges, with a rolled edge stitch and fabric pieces RST, attach a piece of the band to each side of the lace insertion. Press.

- The band piece will now measure 7-8" wide depending on the width of the lace and ladder trim used.

- Trim this strip to the finished width by 40½".

- Cut off 17" of the ribbon.

- Make a mark on the ladder 10¼" from one end.

- Weave the 17" piece of ribbon into the ladder from the same end.

- Weave the remaining ribbon through the ladder from the other end and tie the ribbon pieces together. See page 20 for details on the ladder ribbon and lace insert.

- Trim the remaining band fabric to 8" x 40½".

- Compare the width of the two band pieces.

- Adjust the width of the wider piece to match that of the narrow one.

NOTE: If the outside piece is the one to be adjusted, you will need to take some off each long side to keep the insertion centered in the band.

Construction (CONTINUED)

4-Thread Overlock
Needle: Right, Left
Wave/Overlock: Overlock
Stitch Width: M
Stitch Length: 2.0 - 3.0
Stitch Selector: A
Differential: N (normal)
Foot: Ruffling

- Using a rolled edge stitch, join the short edges of both band pieces RST. Make sure to catch the ends of the ribbon in this seam.

- Thread the serger for 4-thread overlock stitch.

- Adjust this stitch for gathering by increasing the stitch length to 4 and the differential to 2.

- Attach a ruffling foot.

- Gather the unfinished edge of the long 2" wide circle. See page 22 for ruffles and waves technique.

- Return the serger to 4-thread overlock stitch settings.

- Adjust the ruffles to fit the outside edge of the band and attach the ruffle to the band, stitching with RST.

- Stitch the outside and inside band pieces together, sandwiching the ruffle in the seam.

- Turn the band to the outside and press.

- With WST, stitch the unfinished edges of the band. This makes it easier to attach the band to the body of the pillowcase.

- Trim the main body fabric to 27" x 40½".

- With RST, fold in half and serge along the end and side. (Your pillowcase will measure 26¾ x 20.)

- With RST, attach the band to the bottom of the main body. (See page 88.)

- Turn right side out and press.

Ruffles and Ruching Pillow by Pam

Pillow finished size is 12" x 16"
This fun pillow is a great travel size pillow or the perfect lumbar size. It has a ruched center bordered by piping, serger lace, and pleated edges. In this project, you will make each technique before assembling the pillow.

Supplies

- ⅜ yard of fabric for pillow body
- ⅜ yard for pleated ruffle and ruching
- 54" of piping or 1 ½ yards of Micro Welt Cord® and one fat quarter of fabric to make piping
- 17" zipper tape and one slide
- One spool of WonderFil™ Dazzle™ to match fabric
- 12" x 16" pillow form or Pam's Perfect Puff & Stuff®
- Knife Pleat Tape®
- Fabric marker
- Optional: Wonder Clips®
- Optional: Ultimate Pillow Template®
- Optional: Double Stick Tape®
- Hemostats

Construction

Pleats and Ruching Cutting

- Cut pleated/ruching fabric into 4" bias, using the continuous bias method on page 34.

- Cut 40" of bias for the center ruching. Set aside.

Pleats

- Fold the remaining bias in half lengthwise to make the pleated ruffle.

- Place your knife pleat tape near the folded edge.

- Pleat 1" pleats, using directions on the package.

- Make about 28" of pleats so you have an ample amount for both sides, some trimming will be required.

- Set aside. (See page 37 for pleated trim.)

3-Thread Overlock - Wide	
Needle:	Left
Stitch Width:	6.0
Stitch Length:	3.0
Stitch Selector:	A
Differential:	1.0 or N (normal)
Foot:	Curve

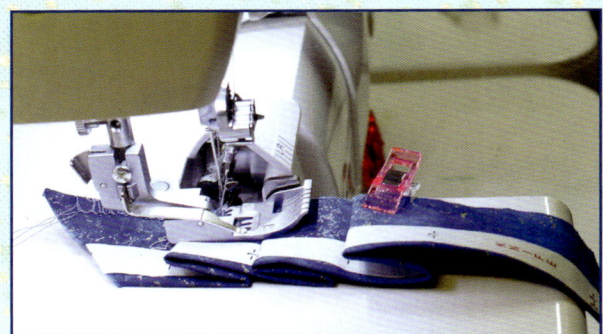

Ruffles and Ruching Pillow (CONTINUED)

Construction (CONTINUED)

Ruching with the Ruffling Foot

- Make the ruching by gathering the fabric on both sides, by using the directions on page 40.

- If ruching needs to be a bit smaller, or more tightly gathered, pull the needle thread to achieve the desired size of 13½".

- Adjust the folds and steam if necessary to make the folds lie smooth.

3-Thread Overlock - Wide
Needle: Left
Stitch Width: 6.0
Stitch Length: 4.0
Stitch Selector: D
Differential: 2.0
Foot: Ruffling

Piping

- If making your own piping, cut your fat quarter into 1½" wide continuous bias (see page 34). You will need a total of 54" of bias and Micro Welt Cord® for this pillow. (See page 36.)

3-Thread Overlock - Wide
Needle: Left
Stitch Width: 6.0
Stitch Length: 3.0
Stitch Selector: D
Differential: 1.0 or N (normal)
Foot: Cording/Piping

Serger Lace

- Cut two pieces of pillow body front 13½" x 8½".

- On each piece, mark a vertical line 1¾" from the edge.

- Mark another vertical line 4½" from the same edge.

- Fold the fabric along the first line you marked and stitch as shown so the upper looper thread will be on top when pressed toward the outside.

3-Thread Overlock - Wide
Needle: Left
Stitch Width: 7.5
Stitch Length: Start out at 1.5 - 2.0 depending on the thickness of your thread
Stitch Selector: A
Differential: 1.0 or N (normal)
Foot: Open Toe
Cutter: Locked

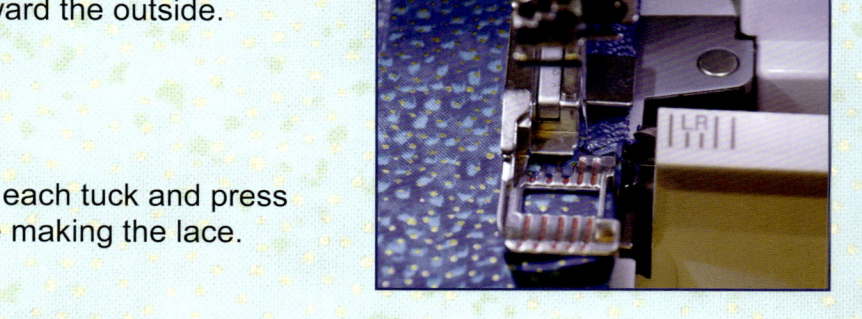

- Stitch each tuck and press before making the lace.

- Follow directions on page 24 for making serger lace.

- Repeat by making the lace on the other three lines marked.

Ruffles and Ruching Pillow (CONTINUED)

Construction (CONTINUED)

Pillow Assembly

3-Thread Overlock - Wide
Needle: Left
Stitch Width: 7.5
Stitch Length: 2.5
Stitch Selector: A
Differential: 1.0 or N (normal)
Foot: Cording/Piping

- Serge piping to each of the inner edges of the pillow fronts with the serger lace.

- Serge ruching to one piped edge.

- Pin or Wonder Clip® ruching to the other piped side, adjusting gathers to make sure they go straight across.

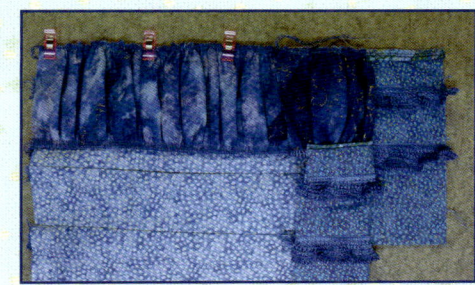

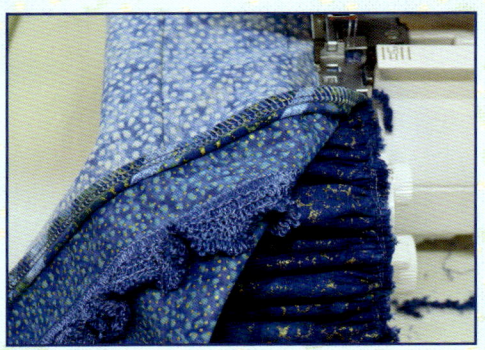

- Serge in place.

Helpful hint: When serging the piped edge to the ruching, serge with the wrong side of piped edge up. If you have a tiny bit (about ⅛") of the ruching extending, it will prevent any stitches showing from the right side.

- Gently press seams from the back side trying not to flatten the ruching or serger lace.

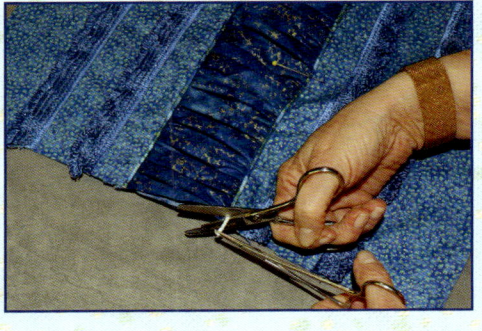

- Trim pillow front to measure 13" x 17", making sure to keep the ruching centered.

- At the ends of each piping piece, use hemostats to pull cord ends out about ⅝" and cut this off. This will make it easier to serger the outer seams.

- Cut the pillow back 13" x 17".

Just For Fun!

Construction (CONTINUED)

Optional

- If you wish to trim the "dog ears" off your pillow, with right sides together, place the Ultimate Pillow Template® on your pillow as shown, lining up with the 12" pillow lines.

  NOTE: Scan this QR code for a video tutorial on how to use the template.

url on page 28

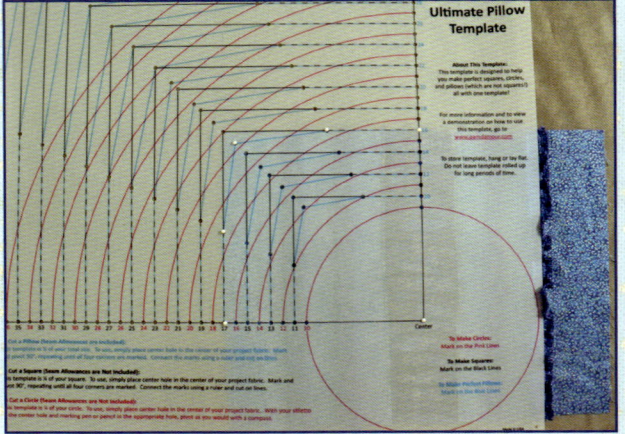

- Mark each corner and trim.

Finishing

Edge Piping

- Add piping to each of the ends of the pillow.

- Pull ⅝" of the cord out at each end, just as you did earlier.

4-Thread Overlock - Wide
Needle: Right, Left
Stitch Width: 6.0
Stitch Length: 3.0
Stitch Selector: A
Differential: 1.0 or N (normal)
Foot: Cording/Piping

Pleated Ruffle

- Finish your pleated trim to 11" by cutting and folding raw edges inside. Use Permanent Double Stick Tape® or fusible web to close ends.

- Fold raw edges in toward the inside, even with the last pleat.

- Use Permanent Double Stick Tape® or fusible web to secure.

- Pin or Wonder Clip® a pleated ruffle to each end.

- Your ruffle should be at least ½" from the raw edge.

Ruffles and Ruching Pillow (CONTINUED)

Finishing (CONTINUED)

4-Thread Overlock - Wide
Needle: Right, Left
Stitch Width: 6.0
Stitch Length: 3.0
Stitch Selector: A
Differential: 1.0 or N (normal)
Foot: Cording/Piping

Zipper Insertion

- Separate your zipper and sew one side to the pillow front bottom and one side to the pillow back bottom. (See page 42.)

- After marrying the zipper together, leave the slide in the center. Do not worry about leaving an opening, because this zipper has a non-locking slide.

Completion

- To complete your pillow, line up the front and back RST with the zipper flat (do not fold the zipper), toward the back side, and serge the remaining three sides together.

  Note: *To reinforce the ends of the zipper, use your regular sewing machine and stitch across the zipper ends before turning right side out.*

Ruffled Jeans by Betty

Ruffles are a perfect addition to almost any garment. They can be added to ready to wear garments, as well as incorporated into the construction of the garments you sew for yourself. While we chose to embellish some denim jeans, just picture these techniques on the bottom of a skirt, as an addition to a sleeve, or running vertically on the front of a shirt or jacket. While the construction techniques for the ruffles are similar, the possibilities for placement are endless!

Supplies

- Garment to embellish
- One or more coordinating fabrics for ruffles and trim (the amount is determined by the number and depth of the ruffles to be used. This is a great way to use WOF 'stash' fabric pieces.)
  Double ruffle uses two strips 4" x WOF and one strip 1" x WOF for trim.
  Chain stitch ruffle jeans uses two strips 2½" x WOF.
- Decorative threads to coordinate with the fabrics
- Serger cone thread to coordinate with the fabrics.
- Ric rac, ribbon or coordinating fabric to cover gathers
- Narrow belt loop binder
- Fabric marker and quilting ruler

Construction of the Double Ruffles

- Cut two strips of fabric 4" x WOF.

url on page 28

- Roll edge stitch one long edge of each strip and gather the other long edge following the directions and stitch settings on page 40 for creating the ruffles.

- Determine the finished length desired for your jeans and trim the legs accordingly.

- At this point, the serger should still be threaded for gathering. Lower the differential to N and the stitch length to 2.5.

- Turn the jeans inside out and stitch around the cut edge of each leg.

- Thread the serger for a cover stitch - center right and attach the cover chain foot.

- Turn under ½" of the ruffle and press.

Cover Stitch - Center Right
Needles: Center, Right
Wave/Overlock: N/A
Stitch Width: N/A
Stitch Length: 2.5 - 3.0
Stitch Selector: N/A
Differential: N (normal)
Foot: Cover Chain
Attach Sewing Table

Just For Fun!

Construction (CONTINUED)

- Attach the first ruffle to the bottom edge of the one leg, covering the overlock stitches on the leg with the gathering stitches on the ruffle.

- When you are just before the point where you started attaching the ruffle, trim the remaining fabric so you have enough to finish plus 1" extra.

- Fold this fabric under and place it on top of the beginning edge of the ruffle.

- Finish stitching the ruffle in place.

- Reposition pants so you can cover stitch on top of the folded fabric from the bottom of the ruffle toward the gathers. Secure the beginning threads using your favorite method.

- Repeat for the other leg.

- Turn right side out to mark for the second ruffle.

- Determine the position of the second ruffle and mark a stitching line.

  NOTE: The amount of offset is part personal preference and part depth of the ruffles. Just make sure there is enough overlap to sufficiently cover the top of the first ruffle.

- Turn the pants inside out and attach the second ruffle in the same manner as the first.

- Thread the serger for cover stitch wide.

- Attach a belt loop binder.

- Using the 1" x WOF strip, follow the directions on page 32 to create a strip of belt loop fabric.

- Center this over the gathering stitches on the top ruffle.

- Stitch in place.

Cover Stitch - Wide	
Needles:	Left, Right
Wave/Overlock:	N/A
Stitch Width:	N/A
Stitch Length:	2.5 - 3.0
Stitch Selector:	N/A
Differential:	N/A
Foot:	Cover Chain
Attach Sewing Table	

- Just before you reach your starting point, trim the strip so you have just enough to cover your beginning stitches and turn under the end ½".

- Continue stitching until you have covered your starting point and overlapped your stitches for 1".

- Repeat for the other leg.

Just For Fun!

Construction of the Ruffle in the Middle

- Thread the serger for the wave stitch with matching decorative threads in the loopers. The sample features Madeira Decor 12.

- Wave stitch both long sides of the 2½" x WOF strips.

- For threading and gathering, follow the directions on page 13 for a chain stitch ruffle.

Wave Stitch
Needles: Right
Wave/Overlock: Wave
Stitch Width: 7.5
Stitch Length: Varies
Stitch Selector: B
Differential: N (normal)
Foot: Utility
Attach Sewing Table

- Ruffle down the center of each strip.

- Determine the finished length of the jeans.

- Trim to desired length plus 1".

- Turn under 1" on each leg and press.

- Thread the serger for cover stitch - right narrow.

- Turn the pants inside out and hem with the narrow cover stitch.

- Place the ruffle on top of the pants so that the lower edge just covers the fold for the hem.

Cover Stitch - Right Narrow
Needles: Center, Right
Wave/Overlock: N/A
Stitch Width: N/A
Stitch Length: 2.5 - 3.0
Stitch Selector: N/A
Differential: N (normal)
Foot: Utility
Attach Sewing Table

> *NOTE: The stitch used to attach the ruffle is determined by the trim being used. If using ribbon or binding, you will use a cover stitch. The width of the stitch (wide or narrow) is determined by the width of the trim. Ric rac is used on the sample. This requires a chain stitch.*

- Convert the serger to chain stitch by removing the right needle, leaving only the center needle in the machine.

- Place the ric rac on top of the gathering stitches and chain stitch down the center of the trim.

- When you near the starting point cut the ric rac leaving just enough to turn under and overlap the beginning.

- Continue stitching for another inch to secure your ends.

> *NOTE: Scan the QR code on page 96 for a video tutorial on how to make ruffled jeans.*

Ruffled Towels   by Betty

The same techniques used on the jeans can be easily applied to items for your home. This is a quick and easy project that can be used as a great gift!

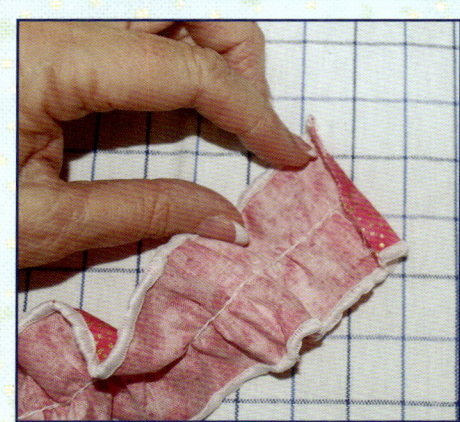

Supplies

- Towel
- Decorative threads
- Fabric strips to ruffle (we just used the leftover fabric from the jeans!)
- Ribbon, fabric strips, or ric rac

url on page 28

Construction

- The directions and stitch settings are identical to the ruffles on the jeans, except for the beginning and end of the strips.

- Double fold the beginning of the strip ½".

- Press.

- Keep the first edge folded and align it with the edge of the towel.

- Place the ruffle in the desired position on the towel and stitch in place.

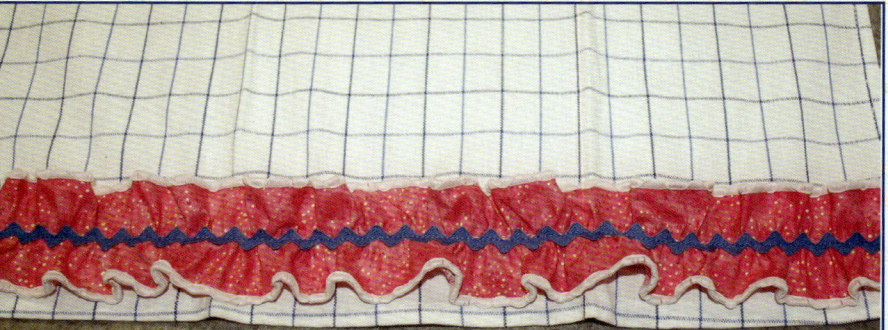

- Trim the remaining ruffle at the end so that you have 1" of extra fabric to make a double ½" fold to match the beginning.

- Secure the stitches at each end with your preferred method.

    NOTE: Scan the QR code at the top of the page for a video tutorial on how to attach the ruffle.

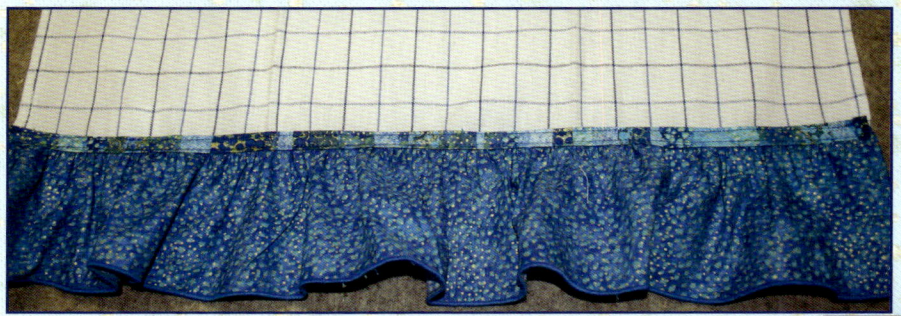

Beaded Serger Necklace by Pam

Any serger with a rolled edge stitch can be used to make this necklace. You can use leftover bits of thread, decorative thread, assorted beads, buttons and/or other findings. Big jewelry is all the rage now, so here's your chance to strut your creativity. Although this concept is not mine, I have been having lots of fun with it and I hope you do too! (Thank you Betty Mitchell for teaching me my first serger necklace!)

Supplies

- Clear fishing line. I used 6 to 15 pound test, or whatever I'm able to sneak out of my husband's tackle box!
- Three spools of thread. You can mix rayon, metallic, decorative, heavy or regular serger thread.
- Assorted beads: 50 to 70 depending on how many strands you want.
- Two jump rings
- One clasp
- Tweezers
- Small needle nose pliers
- Hand sewing needle

url on page 28

Rolled Edge

Needle: Right Overlock
Wave/Overlock: Overlock
Stitch Width: 3.5
Stitch Length: 1 (rolled edge)
Stitch Selector: D
Differential: N (normal)
Foot: Cover/Chain

Construction

- Start by cutting your fishing lines into 36" lengths. You will want them longer than your actual necklace because you lose length when you add each bead. Cut the number of strands you want for your necklace.

- Thread your beads onto the fishing line. Put about 10-12 beads on each line. You may want to knot each end so the beads do not slide off.

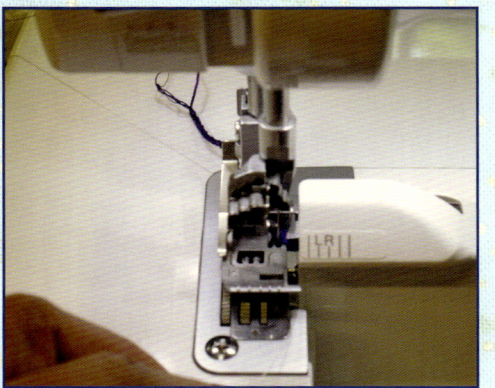

- Thread your serger to a rolled edge. Test your stitch before starting by stitching off a chain.

- Place one end of the fishing line in the stitching path, with about 3" extended and sew a couple of stitches, catching the fishing line. Wrap the end back toward you so that it gets wrapped in the stitches.

Beaded Serger Necklace (CONTINUED)

Construction (CONTINUED)

- Pull the first bead up, looping the fishing line with the bead behind to the right of the machine's ankle. Sew a few stitches, then pull the slack out of the line.

- Repeat this until all the beads are used up. At the end, chain off another 10-12 inches.

NOTE: The common rookie mistake is serging with too much space between the beads and then you run out of fishing line. Do not worry if this happens because when it is all together you will never notice these gaps. You can always make a new strand with the leftover beads or hand sew beads to fill gaps.

- After all your strands are made, it is time to put your necklace together.

- Arrange the strands as desired. One option is to have varying lengths; another is to make them similar lengths and twist. For more fullness, consider adding more strands of serged thread without beads.

- With a hand sewing needle and some of the thread used in the necklace, make a few stitches at the ends to secure all the sections. Draw the ends through the jump ring, wrap over and use the longest serger chain to encase the other ends.

- Trim off all raw ends of serger thread.

- Secure with needle and thread. Finish the other end in the same manner.

- Another way to finish it is by tying the ends together and wrapping any longer tails around to secure it. If you choose this method, you will not need any extra jewelry findings, but you will need to leave the necklace long enough to pull over your head!

- Once you have made your first serger necklace, it is time to scour your stash to see what else you can make into serger jewelry!

NOTE: *Scan the QR code on the previous page for a video tutorial on how to make a beaded serger necklace.*

Remember: Recycle, Repurpose and Reap the compliments! Here are some other design options.

Some ideas are: *old bobbins, wooden spools, buttons, sea shells, keys, zipper tabs, and old jewelry parts such as odd earrings, pendants, and old charms. If you can put a hole in it, you can use it!*

Serger Headband by Pam

This darling headband can be made for both children and adults. It's a great way to use up your decorative threads. The embroidered flower covers where the ends of the headband are joined together. To make this embroidered flower, go to this QR link and download the file. If you don't have an embroidery machine, a silk flower from your favorite craft supply store will do nicely. I used colored fold over elastic, but if it's not available where you are, soft ¼" lingerie elastic can be used.

Supplies

Embroidered Flower
- ½ yard of polyester or nylon sheer fabric
- Texture Magic™ or other "shrinking fabric"
- One spool of Lamé Stylo Thread 🧵 or other decorative embroidery thread

url on page 28

Headband
- 1½ yard of fold over elastic, or 3 yards of ¼" soft lingerie elastic
- One spool of WonderFil™ Razzle™
- One Spool of WonderFil™ Spaghetti™
- One spool of sewing or serger thread
- Basting tape 🧵

Construction

- Cut a two-inch length of elastic and set it aside.

- If using fold over elastic, cut down the center to make two lengths.

- With your serger set up for a 3-thread overlock - wide, serge over the elastic, trimming off any excess (see page 33). Always test your stitch first to make sure your settings are right for your thread and elastic. You may have to lengthen or shorten your stitch to create a satin stitch.

3-Thread Overlock - Wide	
Needle: Left	
Stitch Width: 6.0	
Stitch Length: 2.0	
Stitch Selector: A	
Differential: N (normal)	
Foot: Curve Foot	

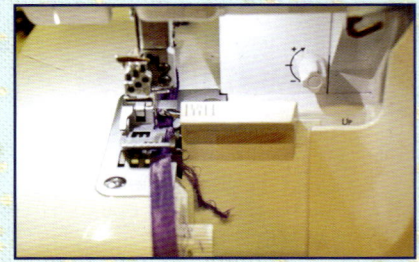

- Stitch over all your elastic and cut into four pieces.

- Place basting tape on the two-inch piece of elastic, and line up all four pieces.

Just For Fun!

Construction (CONTINUED)

- Serge across the ends of the four pieces of trim you just made.

- Begin your head band by weaving your four pieces of trim, pinning it into your pressing surface to anchor it. Begin on one side and weave the tail in and out of the other trims.

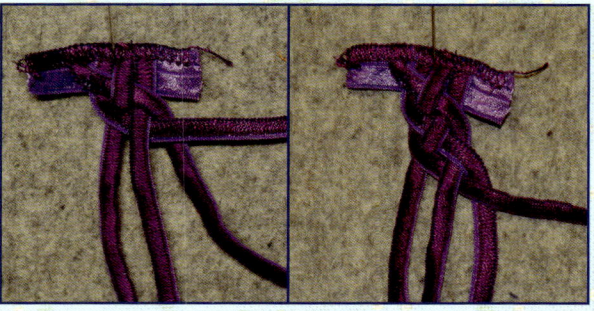

- Continue to weave in and out, starting with the section on the same side each time.

- Pin the end so it does not come apart and fit to size. Wrap the elastic ends around the beginning end and sew in place to secure. You may need to sew this on your regular sewing machine.

Embroidered Flower

- Using the file from the QR code on the previous page, embroider three flowers with two layers of sheer fabric, and three flowers with the Texture Magic™ (or shrinking fabric) between two layers of sheer fabric using the same thread top and bottom.

- To avoid excess thickness in the center of the flower, advance through the design so that you do not stitch the flower centers on the non-shrinking flowers.

- With your iron set on steam, hover over the shrinking flowers, until they are the size you want. Here are three flowers partially steamed to shrink to different sizes.

- Layer the flowers with the progressively smaller ones on top of the others.

- Sew the flowers onto your headband over the spot where the ends were joined.

Baby Bunting by Pam

Whenever I want to give a baby gift, I always make my own receiving bunting blanket to use as the gift wrap. It's more economical than buying wrapping paper, and it's like two gifts in one!

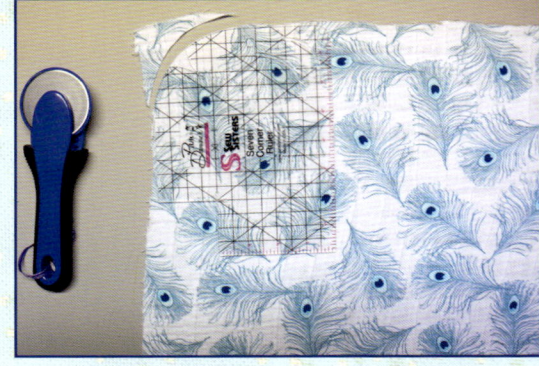

Supplies

- 1¼ yards of soft fabric, such as flannel or double gauze. (we used Plumage Embrace® Teal double gauze)
- Two spools of wooly nylon or wooly poly thread
- One cone of serger thread
- 7 Corner Ruler® by the Sew Sisters

Construction

- Trim your fabric so that it is square. Most fabrics are 42" to 45" wide, so after trimming off the selvages, cut the length to the same size as the width.

- With the 7 Corner Ruler®, trim each corner using the 3" curve. If you do not have the 7 Corner Ruler®, cut a gentle curve on one corner, and use it as your pattern for the remaining corners.

- With your serger set up for a 3-thread rolled edge, serge all the way around, starting and stopping along one of the straight edges.

3-Thread Rolled Edge
Needle: Right
Wave/Overlock: Overlock
Stitch Width: M
Stitch Length: 1.5 - 2.0
Stitch Selector: D
Differential: N (normal)
Foot: Curve Foot

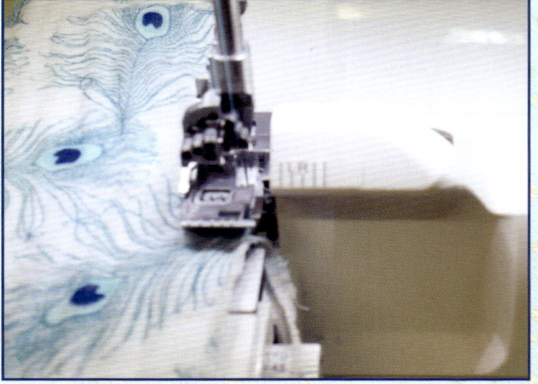

- When you get back to where you started, overlap stitching by an inch, lift your presser foot, pull threads out, and trim. Add fray block if needed.

Acknowledgements

Thank you to the following companies who provided us with support through their products and machines. We hope you will thank these companies by supporting them.

FOR THE LOVE OF SEWING

Glossary

NOTE: You will find terms here that are not in this book, but I included them so you could use this as a reference guide for all your sewing projects.

4-thread overlock stitch: A balanced stitch where the two looper threads meet at the cut edge of the fabric. When the tensions are properly balanced you will not see either looper thread wrap to the opposite side of the fabric. This stitch is meant for construction and should not be used on a single layer of fabric.

3-thread overlock - wide stitch: A balanced stitch where the looper threads meet at the cut edge of the fabric and do not overlap onto the opposite side of the fabric. The right needle is removed for this stitch. The most common use of the 3 thread overlock -wide is for decorative edging using heavier threads in both loopers.

3-thread overlock - narrow stitch: A balanced stitch where the two looper threads meet at the cut edge of the fabric. When the tensions are properly balanced you will not see either looper thread wrap to the opposite side. This stitch is most often used to finish the edges of garment seams. It may also be used for garment construction when fine, light weight, fabrics are used.

3-thread rolled edge: This is 3 thread narrow stitch. It is not a balanced stitch. The upper looper tension is decreased while the lower looper thread tension is increased. This allows the upper looper thread to roll over to the back of the fabric and cover the lower looper thread. The stitch length is usually very short allowing the entire edge of the fabric to be covered with thread. This stitch is often referred to as the 'napkin edge'. It is also used to finish the edge of scarves and is frequently used to seam delicate garments such as lingerie and heirloom style garments.

Basting: Temporary stitches used to create gathers, or to temporarily sew something together. The stitches are usually 3.5 - 4.5mm in length and are taken out when the project is completed.

Bias: If something is cut on the true bias, it is cut at 45° to the selvage, or on a diagonal line across the fabric.

Bias Band: A strip of fabric cut on the bias and applied onto another fabric.

Binding: A method for finishing edges or seams by wrapping fabric over the edge to encase the raw edges.

Cover and chain stitches: Not all sergers have these capabilities. They require the serger to have an additional looper to create the stitches. They are most frequently used for hems, single rows of stitches that look like a traditional machine stitch on the top of the fabric, or for decorative purposes when heavier threads are used in the chain stitch looper. Sergers with cover and chain capabilities traditionally have three needle positions. Chain stitch, which uses only one needle, can then be stitched in the left, center or right needle position. The stitches will look the same regardless of the needle position. The primary benefit of the different positions is that you have choices for stitch placement relative to some other marking or stitch line on your project.

Cover stitch: It is easily identified as the stitch that is used in hemming ready to wear t-shirts. Cover stitch can be done with two or three needles. A triple cover stitch is most often decorative as it will look like three perfectly placed rows of top stitching on the outside of a garment. A narrow cover stitch will use the center needle position and either the left or right needle position. Narrow cover stitch is the hemming stitch. A wide cover stitch uses the two outside needle positions. It is often used with various attachments or specialty feet. When heavy, decorative threads are used in the chain stitch looper, the cover and chain stitches can be used to enhance or embellish the fabric. Because the decorative thread is in the looper, the right side of the fabric will be face down on the serger and you will be stitching with the wrong side facing you.

Curve Foot: It is short and has a flat bottom which allows you to get close to the needle and control the fabric, such as when stitching curves or sewing across seams.

Fabric Grain: The direction of the fabric, up and down the length or perpendicular to the selvage. They are called the lengthwise grain, crosswise grain and the bias.

Fantastic Fusible Fabric Backing®: This is a 60" wide light weight sheer fusible stabilizer designed to stabilize fabric without changing the hand of the fabric.

Glossary

(CONTINUED)

FriXion® Pen: This pen, not designed for fabric use, is used by many sewists. It gives a crisp line and disappears when ironed. Fabric needs to be washed to remove pen residue.

Hemostats: A locking pair of pliers similar to needle nose. They are usually used as a clamp in the medical field.

Lining: This is a lightweight fabric that lines a project. It prevents lighter weight fabrics from appearing too sheer, as well. Linings can complement the outside fabric or contrast for an exciting inside personality to your project.

Piping: A decorative or covered cording inserted into the seam of a project for decoration. It is also known as welting.

Pivot: Turning a corner or angle while your needle is in the fabric and the presser foot is raised to prevent the fabric layers from shifting apart.

Placket: An extra piece of fabric added to hold a zipper.

Raw Edge: The cut edge of a project. It may fray or ravel if left in this state.

RFID Fabric: This is used to line wallets and bags to prevent thiefs from scanning critical credit card and identity data.

Right Side (RS): Right side, usually in reference to the right side of fabric, which is the side of the fabric with the print or finish.

Right Side Together (RST): Right sides together is a term meaning that two pieces of fabric should have the right sides facing each other before you sew.

Sandwich: The method of layering fabrics, batting, and/or stabilizer together before sewing.

Seam Allowance (SA): The fabric between the cut edge of the project and the seam line. This measurement varies based on the type of project you are doing. This book was written with the standard 1/2" seam allowances, unless otherwise specified.

Seam Ripper: A sewer's best friend! It is used to remove basting stitches as well as "accidents".

Selvage: The woven edge of the fabric. One of the selvages usually has printing on it.

Stiletto: This tool is your "third hand" when sewing. It is very sharp and can hold your fabric in place as you sew. It will not damage the fabric.

Stitch Length (SL): The length of the stitch.

Straight Grain: The direction of the threads traveling parallel to the selvage.

Super Shaping Foam®: By The Decorating Diva, Super Shaping Foam comes 60" wide and can be purchased as single sided fusible or double sided fusible.

Top Stitching: This is a decorative stitch like edge stitching, but further from the edge of the garment. It can be done in multiple rows and looks very pretty.

WOF: Width of fabric

Wonder Clips®: These clips, by Clover, take the place of pins and are great for holding fabric edges together. They come in assorted sizes to accommodate different weights of fabrics.

Wrong Side (WS): Wrong side usually refers to the wrong side of fabric. This side of the fabric is bland and usually has a muted version of the printed side of the fabric.

Wrong Sides Together (WST): Wrong sides together means that the two fabrics that are to be sewn together have their wrong sides touching.

Index

Index

Products List

The following are available at www.pamdamour.com

- 5-in-1 Ruler® by Pam Damour
- 7 Corner Ruler® by the Sew Sisters
- 7½" Wallet Clasps
- 48" Bag Chain
- Basting Tape
- Brass Seam Ripper
- Brass Stiletto
- Box Pleat Tape® by Pam Damour
- Continuous Bias Guide® by Pam Damour
- Double Sided Basting Tape
- Fantastic Fusible Fabric Backing®
- Flex & Firm®
- FriXion® Pen
- Knife Pleat Tape® by Pam Damour
- Lamé Stylo Thread
- Magic Fabric Crayon®
- Micro Stitch™ Basting Gun
- Micro Welt Cord®
- Permanent Double Stick Tape®
- Pocket Peel & Stick Stabilizer®
- Pam's Perfect Puff & Stuff®
- Size 00 Phillips Head Screwdriver
- Small Wallet Clasps
- Snip It Scissors
- Standard Welt Cord®
- Super Shaping Foam® (Comes in Single or Double Side Fusible)
- Valance Welt Cord®
- Wonder Clips®
- Zipper Tape and Slides